The day is December 2, 1804—Josephine Bonaparte is crowned Empress of France during the famous coronation of Napoleon. One of Josephine's court ladies has begun an account of the lavish event in her memoirs with these words:

. . . The great golden coach, drawn by eight bay horses and surmounted by a crown and four spread-winged imperial eagles, passed through the gates of the Tuileries Palace, the Emperor and Empress seated on its white velvet cushions.

Such fascinating accounts derived from memoirs, documents and personal letters are found throughout *More Than A Queen, the story of Josephine Bonaparte,* allowing the reader the most personal glimpse of this romantic and colorful historical figure.

Recreating her life from that strange prophecy of her childhood—"A queen . . . *more* than a queen!"—through both an exciting and sorrowful life as Empress, and then into her seclusion at Malmaison, Frances Mossiker looks deeply into the character of Josephine.

MORE THAN A QUEEN

the story of
Josephine Bonaparte

by Frances Mossiker

drawings by Michael Eagle

Alfred A. Knopf · New York

This is a Borzoi Book
Published by Alfred A. Knopf, Inc.

Copyright © 1971 by Frances Mossiker

All rights reserved under International
and Pan-American Copyright Conventions.
Published in the United States
by Alfred A. Knopf, Inc., New York,
and simultaneously in Canada
by Random House of Canada Limited, Toronto.
Distributed by Random House, Inc., New York.

Trade Edition: ISBN: 0–394–82049–5
Library Edition: ISBN: 0–394–92049–x

Library of Congress Catalog Card Number: 74–131386
Manufactured in the United States of America

for
PAULA LANDESMAN
with love

MORE THAN A QUEEN

the story of Josephine Bonaparte

PART
I

The rough, wrinkled, black hand clasped the soft, smooth, white one, and curled back the tapering fingers to read the lines of the palm.

Euphémie, the old Negro slave woman, was the most famous fortune-teller of the Caribbean island of Martinique, and the four young girls had slipped away from home during the siesta hour—when nothing stirred but the hammocks—to come to Euphémie's rickety palm-thatched shack in the grove of golden-yellow acacia trees to ask her what the future held in store for them.

Suddenly, the old woman, sitting crossed-legged on her reed mat on the dirt floor, jerked up straight and searched the face of the girl whose hand she held. She then began to gabble so fast and furiously in the strange slave dialect—a jumble of French and tribal African—that Marie-Josèphe-Rose de Tascher de la Pagerie and her two sisters and their friend could scarcely understand a word she said.

Yeyette—Marie-Josèphe-Rose's nickname—looked anxiously

into her own small pink palm to see what had excited the fortune-teller. She could see only wriggly, feathery lines running every which way, though mostly crosswise. She certainly had not studied the science of palmistry, could not tell the life line from the head line from the line of fate, and did not know that the fleshy pad just under the thumb was called the Mount of Venus, and told the palmist whether one's heart was warm or cold, chilly or affectionate. Euphémie had never read any books on the subject of palmistry either, but she was supposed to have "second sight," the power to see into the shadowy future as into a dark and cloudy glass.

"Euphémie, what do you see?" Yeyette asked impatiently. "Is it good or bad? Tell me, tell me!"

"Bad *and* good, both, Mademoiselle. Some happy things, some unhappy. The unhappy, first. You will sail across the seas to marry and have children, but that marriage will end in sorrow, with your husband's death . . . a terrible death such as no one has ever died before." (The old woman's voice rose to a wail and her eyes rolled back in her head.)" . . . Your children to be left fatherless and you, a widow. But you will marry again, and then . . . *then,* become a queen!" Euphémie rolled her eyes back down again and rubbed them, drawing Yeyette's hand closer still, as if she could not believe what she saw there. "A queen . . . *more* than a queen!" she shrieked.

"Nonsense!" Yeyette exclaimed, rushing out of the dark

little hut into the blinding afternoon sun, the other girls blinking and following behind her. Why, the Cinderella story was easier to believe than this one! Could the old witch be teasing her? "Queen" of *what*? And what could she mean by "*more than a queen*"? Who could be more of a queen than the new Queen of France, the lovely young Marie Antoinette, whose portrait everyone was admiring, queenly to her fingertips, born to wear a crown, daughter of an Austrian empress, wife of a Bourbon king, Louis XVI, sixteenth Louis in the long line of French kings? How could a little nobody of an island girl expect to take a position such as Marie Antoinette's on the throne of France, to become a queen as Euphémie had foretold? Kings were born as sons of kings, the wives of kings became queens, but kings married only princesses of royal blood, like themselves. Euphémie's prediction that Yeyette would, one day, wear a crown was absurd, ridiculous, nonsensical! The world would have to be turned upside down, all the rules would have to be changed for such a thing to happen.

The world *would* be turned upside down, and when it was the historians would call it the French Revolution. But no one would have believed Euphémie, in the 1770's, if she had predicted a republic replacing a monarchy, a bloody end to kings and queens, all twenty years before it happened.

Yeyette's companions shook their heads in puzzlement at the predictions Euphémie had made, yet none of them dared laugh aloud at the fortune-teller, who could cast a spell as easily as she could read the lines of a palm.

Yeyette shrugged, and led the others down a palm-lined path to the Point. There was a wonderful place to swim and to watch the horizon for the great white sails that marked French royal naval vessels on their way across the Bay to Fort-Royal—called Fort-de-France on the map today, capital of the French colony of Martinique.

Upon the arrival of a corvette, a frigate, or a battleship—and Yeyette could tell which was which a mile away—she could expect an invitation from her uncle, the Baron de Tascher, commander of the port, to come to visit and to dance at the balls honoring the gallant young naval officers. Some officers were old friends; some, new; all smartly uniformed, all eager to come ashore, to meet the young ladies of Martinique who enjoyed a reputation as women of great beauty. It was a distinction for which they had Columbus to thank, his sailors having brought back to Spain stories of sirens sighted in the Antilles—mermaids with coral hair and the scales of their fishtails flashing brighter than sequins through the blue waters of the Caribbean.

Yeyette was not yet a siren, but she had chestnut curls—brown with a trace of red in them—and magnolia-petal skin. The color of her eyes must have changed color with the color of the dress she wore, for some observers spoke of her blue eyes, others called them brown, and still others, hazel. Perhaps it was because her lashes were so long and dark that they half-concealed her eyes. She was not tall, nor would she grow much taller—five feet, or thereabouts. In her early teens she was quite pretty, though not as pretty as she would become a few years later, for she eventually grew slender as a reed and graceful as a willow.

The French fleet weighed anchor often in Fort-Royal harbor, although it never seemed often enough to Yeyette and her friends. With France and England at war or on the brink of war over their New World colonies throughout so much of the eighteenth century, the French navy regularly patrolled its possessions in the West Indies. Its vessels sailed especially between the family of islands known as the Lesser—or French—Antilles, including Guadeloupe in the Leeward Isles, and Martinique, Sainte Lucie, and Grenade in the Windward Isles, poetically called les Iles-sous-le-Vent, by the French, which means literally the Isles-under-the-Wind.

Not only Yeyette, but all the other young island girls lived for the gay times at Fort-Royal—the Mardi Gras week festivities and the gala days when the fleet came in. As bright-hued as tropical birds, the young ladies flocked—though they did not fly—into the capital in their gaily colored muslin and cotton dresses. They came by boat, by carriage, by horse, and even, from nearby plantations, by hammock, with a pair of slaves to carry them.

Yeyette usually came by pirogue, the light and swift native canoe hollowed out of a log. It was little more than an hour's trip for her from Trois Ilets across Fort-Royal Bay, through one of the most beautiful land and seascapes in the world. By road, the trip took many hours: up, down, and around mountainsides, past extinct volcanoes, across bridges over streams and rivers, through lush green valleys and alongside dark, tangled rain forests, noisy with birds, dripping with wild orchids.

Whether by land or by sea, Yeyette could never get there soon enough: neither the carriage nor the boat traveled quickly enough to suit her, as her heart raced on ahead to Fort-Royal. It was a wonder that she had never tipped the canoe in her excitement, leaning this way and that to catch the first sight of La Savane, the Savannah, that palm- and flower-decked park or esplanade that ran the length of the harbor, behind the wharves and piers. It was the favorite promenade of the townspeople as well as the visitors.

The town of Fort-Royal climbed up the side of Mount Carbet, its houses clinging to the steep, narrow streets. There was the governor's mansion and the government buildings—customs office, courthouse, and jail—to see and to admire, and, best of all, the shops displaying alluring French imports: the

10

latest books of Paris fashions, Paris frocks, fans, feathers, frills, Paris perfumes and rouges.

Yeyette would have bought everything in sight, if only she could. And one day, she could and would—all the beautiful things she laid her eyes on. She had an eye for beauty, and flawlessly good taste.

Fort-Royal may have struck the European visitor as a small, dull, backwater colonial town, but, for Yeyette, it offered all the sights and sounds, all the thrill of a city.

And a city it was, compared to her native Trois Ilets, a cluster of fifty-odd ramshackle wooden houses about a single church. The village of Trois Ilets, Three Islets, took its name from the three small islands just off the shore, each just large enough to hold a tree or two and a couple of boulders. They were odd little snippets of land in the blue water, all the same size but each a slightly different shape; and each with a name of its own: Charles, Sixtain, and Tebloux.

The La Pagerie Plantation—taking its name from Yeyette's family—lay a little more than a mile from the village of Trois Ilets, its fields planted in coffee and tobacco, but mostly in sugar cane, the most profitable crop of the West Indies. A hundred or more slaves, under the whip of a slave-driver, planted and harvested the crops, labored in the sugar mill, hauling in the stalks, feeding them into the rollers to be crushed, collecting and processing the juices, sacking the raw sugar as it was produced.

11

When Yeyette was born, the first child of the family, on June 23, 1763, it was a fine wooden house, covered with wine-red bougainvillea, built around a pleasant courtyard and surrounded by a broad gallery or veranda, open to the breeze, a favorite spot for islanders on hot summer nights. But the terrible hurricane of 1766, the worst in island history, shook the de Tascher home to its foundations.

Yeyette could never be sure whether she really remembered that dreadful August night when four hundred and forty people lost their lives or whether she remembered hearing her mother and father and her mulatto nurse, Marion, tell about it. Marion, superstitious like most islanders, said the sun had sunk into the sea that afternoon in a fearful red blaze, that it "had set in blood," as a Carib witch-doctor described it when he predicted the coming storm. The church bells could be heard sounding the alarm all the way from Trois Ilets, and the de Tascher family—Yeyette, her parents, and her eleven month-old sister, Catherine-Désirée—found shelter just in time, in the solidly built sugar mill, with its stone walls two feet thick. All night they listened to the sounds of destruction going on outside: the crash of trees and thunder, the pounding of the waves. The next morning, they fearfully crept out to discover the terrible damage.

Yeyette's father could never manage to scrape up the money for the repair of the big house. Instead, the two-story sugar mill was remodeled, a gallery added on the south side, and, from the time of the hurricane, became the family home. It was there the third daughter, Marie-Françoise—Manette, for short—was born, not long after.

Yeyette's father could not hide his disappointment that the third child was not a son. Three daughters meant three dowries —the wedding gift of cash or land which the bride's parents were expected to provide for each daughter if they hoped to find a suitable husband for her. Three dowries would mean a terrible hardship for this father, who had never made a fortune in the New World, as he—and his father before him—had hoped to do. The de Tascher family could proudly trace its ancestors back for hundreds of years—knights in shining armor on crusade in the Holy Land, captains in the service of all the kings of France, lords and masters in their Loire River valley domains in the south of France—a noble family and an old one, but not a rich one. Yeyette's grandfather, like so many Frenchmen in the eighteenth century, had sailed away to try his luck in the newly established French colonies in the West Indies. His luck had proved none too good, and that of his son, Yeyette's father, little better.

If the de Taschers were not rich, still, life at La Pagerie Plantation was an easy, pleasant one: their table was heaped high with good things from their gardens, their orchards, their river (called La Pagerie too), and their sea—or rather, that

13

stretch of the Caribbean just beyond their shoreline. The Fruits-
of-the-Sea, as the French call seafood, were abundant and deli-
cious. The "Habitants," giant Martinique prawns or shrimp,
and the red land crabs were served with rice, and highly sea-
soned with native herbs and spices. Simply by reaching up—or
climbing—anyone could pick his fill of bananas, oranges, and
coconuts. The sweetest and juiciest variety of pineapple was
called "France": "France" meant the best; to the French colo-
nials' way of thinking, certainly to Yeyette's, everything French
was superb. Dairy products were supplied in plenty by the La
Pagerie herd of cows. Meat and poultry came from La Pagerie's
own sheep, goats, hogs, and chickens. La Pagerie made up a
little world of its own, sufficient unto itself, supplying most of
its own needs. Even shut off from the rest of the world, the
plantation could have managed quite well on its own.

But La Pagerie was not shut off from the rest of the world,
nor did it want to be: the planters of Martinique were all very
sociable, very hospitable. There was much visiting back and
forth between the large, isolated plantations. Friends and family paid visits to La Pagerie; then the visits were paid back:
Monsieur and Madame from La Pagerie, the three girls with
their maids and nurses, traveled to all corners of the island.

There were trips to Fort-Royal and to Saint Pierre, the large
commercial port at which most of the imports were received
from Europe, where most of the exports—sugar and tobacco,

above all—were loaded for shipment to the mother country, France.

Martinique was not very large: only forty miles long and fifteen miles wide, but it was full of many natural wonders. The island could boast more scenic splendors than were to be seen in some areas ten times as broad: mountain ranges, with their foothills in the water, rising to a summit with the clouds; Diamond Rock, always a visitors' attraction, a giant slab of granite sparkling brighter than a thousand carats in the sea spray; even a live volcano, Mount Pelée, smoking and rumbling from time to time, muttering a constant threat.

Closer to home, Yeyette and her sisters explored on their little island ponies, a breed called Porto Ricans. Their maids and nurses tagged along behind, except on rare occasions when the girls gave them the slip, as on the day they went to consult the fortune-teller, Euphémie. They were used to being waited on hand and foot, and usually wanted Marion and Brigitte, another of their maids, along to carry their carafes of orangeade and picnic baskets, their towels and combs and mirrors, their fishing nets and lines. The slaves also taught the children how to catch the land crabs before they scuttled off to safety in the water, how to fish the streams for the silvery coffer-fish, first prize of the island waters.

Another thing they taught Yeyette, Manette, and Catherine-

Désirée was how to wind and tie the brightly striped Madras bandannas around their heads in enchanting fashions. The knotting and tying was really a set of signals for sweethearts: a knot at one end meant that the wearer's heart was free; two knots in the bandanna signified a heart ready to be won; three knots, a heart already spoken for, already promised; four knots announced a heartless flirt.

When it came to story-telling, their nurses had no equal, and the story-telling hour usually came just before the siesta. The blazing hot afternoon tropical sun set hammocks swaying all over the Caribbean, but the de Tascher girls refused to lie down in theirs until they heard a story, one of the hundreds of wonderful-terrible stories brought from the homeland in Africa. Handed down from one generation to the next, they were stories about strange, dark, jungle gods—snake gods, crocodile gods, horned gods—and about their priests, the witch-doctors, and the magic they could make, voodoo, with all its fearsome charms and harms. Stories about zombies, the walking dead, rising up out of their graves at the bidding of the witch-doctors, were enough to give little girls nightmares; however, they woke up and begged for more.

After the siesta hour was over, the girls and their maids took a ten-minute walk from the house, along a path bordered by pink and yellow hibiscus. There Marion and Brigitte sat on the river bank, fanning away clouds of mosquitoes and keeping watch, while the girls swam in the deep, clear pool formed by the river at its widest point. That same lovely ring of water in the La Pagerie River is now called The Queen's Lake in honor of the girl who, history books say, swam there two hundred and more years ago in her magnolia-petal skin, nothing more, along with her sisters and attendants.

It is a good guess to say that Yeyette, living in France in later life, always thought fondly of her childhood in Martinique, of her friends and family and associates there: anyone from Martinique traveling to France could be sure of a warm welcome. She must have remembered how the slaves pampered and petted her as a little girl; as a woman, she would send to Martinique for her personal attendants. Her household would always include at least one islander wearing a flowered cotton gown and a striped bandanna wound around her head, Creole style. One of them was even with her when she died. Nurse Marion, who held her at her christening, was not forgotten, as the records prove. Marion was eventually freed from slavery and awarded a pension.

Though Yeyette's father may have wished for a son, he was quite fond of his daughters, especially of Yeyette, who never tired of listening to his tales. And one he never tired of telling was about the trip he had made, as a boy of seventeen, to France and the great palace of Versailles, that thousand-windowed gold and marble residence of the kings of France, set in hundreds of acres of park and forest, amid pools and fountains—fifteen hundred water spouts in the fountains, fifteen hundred servants in the palace—one of the wonders of the world.

Boys of noble family were sometimes privileged to serve as pages to the royal family, and Yeyette's father had had the honor of spending several years at court in the household of the wife of the Dauphin, the eldest son and heir apparent of King Louis XV. Joseph de Tascher had been at Versailles the day the Dauphiness had given birth to the boy who, because of his father's early death, came to the throne in 1774 as King Louis XVI.

Sailing ships had recently brought to the colonies the first portraits of the newly crowned young monarch and his wife: the King was not much to look at, even in his gold-embroidered, ermine-trimmed, bejewelled coronation robes, but his radiantly lovely queen, Marie Antoinette, dazzled all eyes, including Yeyette's.

Yeyette could never hear enough about the French royal family, about Versailles, about Paris. Paris was the city of her dreams; she was homesick for it before she ever set foot inside the walls and, once she had lived there, she never willingly left.

For a while, it seemed she might go there very young, as a schoolgirl. From earliest childhood there was talk of her being sent to France to her Aunt Edmée Renaudin who lived there, and had offered to give her niece the advantages of a European education, if her parents would only send or bring the girl across the Atlantic.

Aunt Edmée had gone to France several years earlier with the Beauharnais family. She had met them in Martinique when the Marquis de Beauharnais went there to serve as governor and lieutenant-general of the Windward Isles. The governor's wife, Madame Beauharnais, had invited Edmée Renaudin to join their household as a friend and companion. When the Beauharnais's son, Alexandre, was born in 1760, Edmée was named his godmother and helped to raise the boy; theirs was a relationship which grew closer still after his mother died.

Letters went back and forth between Paris and Trois Ilets on the matter of Yeyette's trip to France. A stack of family letters proves it: the paper is yellow and crumbly, the ink faded, but you can still read the words written in 1766, two centuries ago, by the mother of the three-year-old girl to the girl's aunt. "She shows great promise," Yeyette's mother wrote, "and I hope that in two years' time, you will help her to take advantage of it."

But 1766 was also the year of the hurricane, and by the time the slave quarters, the storehouses and the barns at La Pagerie Plantation were rebuilt there was no money to spare for luxuries such as education or foreign travel.

Even so, in 1768, they were still hoping to find a way to send Yeyette to France. Yeyette's grandmother wrote to Aunt Edmée that year, saying: "You asked for my eldest granddaughter. I am truly not in a position to send her. . . . But I do not despair of being able to accomplish what you wish."

What a shame to miss such a wonderful opportunity! What a disappointment for the child herself, hearing it discussed a hundred times by her parents, grandparents, cousins, aunts, and uncles . . . her hopes raised high one year, dashed the next. Maybe . . . Perhaps . . . We'll see . . . Just wait . . . Later on . . . Yes . . . No . . . How sad . . . Too bad!

In 1772, at the age of nine, it was high time for Yeyette to begin her schooling, if not in Paris, then in Fort-Royal at the Ladies of Providence Convent where she would have instruction in the catechism, in deportment, in penmanship, in drawing and embroidery, in dancing and music—not much of an education by twentieth-century standards, but all the accomplishments considered necessary or suitable for an eighteenth-century female. "Teach your pupils simple, unaffected manners," the nuns were instructed by the bishop. "Affectations spoil the best natural qualities. Since dancing helps to give them an attractive manner and bearing, you need not hesitate to provide a master for them, so long as you are discreet in your selection." The sisters' selection was Monsieur François, the ballet master of the Saint Pierre Theater. Monsieur Frobisseur, the

20

drawing master, was a well-known island artist, a painter of miniatures. If only he had painted this pupil from Trois Ilets instead of teaching her, we might have had an idea of what Yeyette looked like as a girl just entering her teens. As it is, the first known portrait shows her in her thirties.

There were no report cards for pupils of the Fort-Royal Convent, but the girl who got black marks in her studies was obliged to tie black ribbons in her hair, while white ribbons were worn proudly as a sign of scholastic achievement. Since no mention was made in the family letters at the time, there is no way of knowing now about Yeyette's class standing.

As young as she was, Yeyette would not have been homesick at the convent in Fort-Royal, because her grandmother and aunt and uncle lived there, and she must have visited often at their home. And surely there were many holidays during the year when she made the trip across the Bay to Trois Ilets to see her parents and her sisters.

By the time she was fourteen, her convent days were over, and she returned home to La Pagerie Plantation. After that, there was no more talk about schooling abroad; whatever money her family could accumulate would have to go—not into an education—but into dowries for the three de Tascher girls. And heaven only knew how so much as one dowry could ever be gotten together at La Pagerie . . . much less three!

In the eighteenth century, it was not at all unusual for a girl to become engaged at age thirteen or fourteen. At fourteen or fifteen, if she was still without a suitor, a young lady of Martinique might well begin to worry about being an old maid. Yeyette celebrated her fourteenth birthday in 1777, and she too began to worry, as did her family. Her hand was spoken for in every dance at the Fort-Royal parties, but not her hand in marriage. Dance partners by the dozens, but no serious suitors.

It was in 1777 that another letter from Aunt Edmée arrived at Trois Ilets and set off the greatest commotion since the hurricane. Addressed to her brother, the girls' father, it contained the most dazzling proposition imaginable for one of the three de Tascher sisters. An offer—not of schooling—but of marriage.

And what a marriage! To Aunt Edmée's godson, Alexandre de Beauharnais. What a fiancé! with both a title—that of Vicomte in French, Viscount in English—and a fortune: a townhouse in Paris, a château near Blois in the fertile Loire River valley, the source of rich yearly revenue; and in the New World, prosperous plantations in Santo Domingo, at that time called Saint Domingue and still a part of the French empire.

A girl's parents could ask no more, and in the eighteenth century, neither the girl nor the boy, but only the parents were consulted in the marriage negotiations. In this case, what girl—had she been consulted—could have asked for more? Here was a true Prince Charming, not only noble and wealthy, but handsome, young, and romantic; seventeen years old, educated by

22

the best tutors and at the best colleges in France and Germany; one of the best horsemen, one of the best dancers of his regiment, a distinguished infantry regiment under the command of the mighty Duke de la Rochefoucauld. "Attractive of both face and form," Aunt Edmée described him. Her godson had "both wit and talent . . . all the good qualities of heart and soul are united in his character. . . . He is loved by all who know him."

Enough to set a girl's heart to fluttering—but at La Pagerie Plantation it was not one, but three hearts fluttering! For, the terms of the marriage contract were clearly stated: no dowry was required, another cause for rejoicing at Trois Ilets. And the fiancé was clearly indicated. It was the identity of the bride that was in doubt. Which of the three sisters would be chosen?

Shortly after, the Marquis de Beauharnais addressed Monsieur de Tascher by letter dated October 23, 1777; all very formal and very proper, he confirmed the offer: "My son's devotion and respect for Madame Renaudin have aroused his ardent desire to be united in marriage to one of her nieces."

This was the truth, but not quite all of it. According to French law at that time, Alexandre would remain a minor—he could not act independently of his father—for another four years, until his twenty-first birthday. But as a married man, he would come immediately into his legal majority and the control of his mother's estates. So, of course, he was eager to achieve the wedded state, and therefore on the look-out for a bride. It stood to reason that his godmother would more willingly assist him in this purpose if one of her three nieces were to benefit by the arrangement. It was true, as his father said, that Alexandre dearly loved and respected his godmother: "You have taken the place of a mother in my life," he wrote in one of his letters to her, "and I could not love you more tenderly if you were my real mother."

After months of suspense, Alexandre's father wrote to say that his son had expressed a preference among the three de Tascher sisters: "As far as I am concerned, I would have left it to you to decide which daughter is to share the fortune of my son. . . . So that I am expressing not my own but his preference when I herewith request the hand of your second daughter, whose age is best suited to his. . . . Had only your eldest daughter been a year or so younger, she would surely have been our choice since she appears to be, from all description, equally desirable and attractive as a bride. But I must admit that my son, who is only seventeen and a half years old, finds that a young lady of fifteen is of an age too close to his own. This is one of those occasions when understanding parents are forced to yield to circumstances beyond their control."

At last, then, the months of waiting were over, the suspense was at an end, the word was out, the name had been pronounced: it was Catherine-Désirée, aged thirteen, who was to be the Vicomte's bride.

24

Part I

Not Yeyette, the eldest, as might have been expected. And as Yeyette must have anticipated although she never said it aloud, but only in the secret of her heart, in the privacy of her pillow. It must have been a bitter, a shattering disappointment—the prospect of a brilliant marriage, of a glamorous life in Paris, all wiped out by one stroke of the pen.

But if fate ever takes a hand in the affairs of men—and in this girl's life it very often seemed to—now it did.

At the very height of the excitement over the marriage plans, Catherine-Désirée fell ill and died of a tropical fever.

And Yeyette might have begun to hope again, although she would never have admitted it, even to herself. How wicked of her to think of benefiting by her dear little sister's death! But she probably could not stop herself, and then felt she was being punished for her sins when her father wrote to Paris, in January, 1778, to announce the death of the bride-to-have-been and to venture the suggestion that if the eldest girl seemed too old, then perhaps the youngest might not seem too young. Might not the youngest, Manette—Marie-Françoise, the baby of the family —take the place of the second youngest? Eleven and a half was very young, he admitted, but, in one respect, her extreme youth might be considered an advantage: she could be sent to France for a French education, to prepare her properly for marriage to a cultivated and knowledgeable French nobleman and officer. What did the Beauharnais family think of this idea?

Part I

Young Alexandre did not think well of it, at all. If his main purpose in marrying was to hasten to attain his legal majority, to come into immediate control of his own affairs, then he would not welcome the thought of putting it off for a year or more until little Manette reached a marriageable age, such as thirteen or fourteen.

The father of the girls took alarm: he wanted to marry off one of them—no matter which—to this highly eligible suitor.

He returned to a description of his eldest daughter's charms: her ivory velvet complexion, her beautiful eyes, her shapely arms (her legs were just as shapely, although eighteenth-century fathers would not mention their daughters' legs). Yeyette, furthermore, he reminded them, was the one who yearned, who craved, who ardently desired, who madly longed to go to Paris! If the Beauharnais would only reconsider the eldest daughter, she might be the best choice, after all. What would they think of his coming to France in April or May and bringing both girls, so that Alexandre might make his own selection?

Aunt Edmée seized happily upon her brother's suggestion. As long as one of her nieces became the happy bride, she did not care which. With hardly a word of sympathy to spare for poor dear little Catherine-Désirée's death, Aunt Edmée replied to her brother in March of 1778: "We leave you to be guided by providence. Bring us either one of your girls . . . or both! But come, come, I urge you!"

27

Aunt Edmée seemed more eager than the would-be bride-
groom. At the time, he was away with his regiment, and leading a very gay life in the loftiest social circles. He was, as one of
his fellow-officers wrote, "one of the most attractive gentlemen
of his time," and he knew it. He was very conceited. He was
winning a reputation as a ladies' man, and keeping a list of the
hearts he collected. Perhaps he was wondering why he had
committed himself to marry a timid, penniless, unfashionable,
uneducated little island girl, when the great ladies of Paris and
the provinces were making such a fuss over him.

Letters took five to six to seven weeks to cross the Atlantic,
depending on the winds in the sails of the vessels that carried
them: whether the winds were favorable or unfavorable,
whether they blew from the east or west or did not blow at
all.

While the next letter from Paris was awaited, the suspense
mounted at Trois Ilets. Yeyette suffered in silence as her father
began a campaign to talk Manette out of her fear of homesick-
ness, should she be chosen.

When he was suddenly called away to duty with the island
militia in its defense preparations against British raiders, his
wife had her turn. She had just lost one child to death, and
could not bear to lose another—to another continent—not even
for the sake of so fine a marriage.

When the father returned from military maneuvers on the

28

island of Sainte Lucie, Manette refused point-blank to be parted from her mother. She was too young, she claimed, and wept wildly to prove it. Not only her mother but her grandmother backed her up in her refusal to stir an inch—much less three thousand miles—from home.

That left Yeyette . . . twice passed over in favor of her younger sisters. If only Alexandre could be persuaded that her age was really quite suitable to his own!

Her father sang her praises, by mail: "She has an exceedingly sweet disposition . . . Her voice is pleasing, she plays quite well on the guitar and, showing a general aptitude for music, she could, with proper instruction, perfect her singing, playing and dancing. . . . What a pity that she did not have the advantages of a French education. . . . If only I had the money," he wrote to his sister, "I would take ship this moment and bring my eldest daughter who burns with impatience to see her beloved aunt."

Yeyette's father's letter and Alexandre's father's letter crossed in mid-Atlantic.

The latter wrote to urge the former to make all possible haste. He expressed the fear that other influences might be brought to bear upon his son, and other brides proposed. It no longer mattered, he said, which daughter Monsieur de Tascher brought with him: "Whichever one you think best suited to my son is the one we want."

And to hurry things along, he enclosed the official marriage bans, the formal announcements of the forthcoming marriage between Alexandre-François-Marie de Beauharnais and . . . and . . . and . . . WHO? The name of the groom had been neatly written in, but the space for the name of the bride was left blank.

It was up to Monsieur de Tascher to write it in.

The name he wrote was: Marie-Josèphe-Rose! The least likely candidate had won out over the two early choices. It was Yeyette, after all, who wound up the winner.

The marriage bans were posted at the Trois Ilets Church, read aloud to the small congregation three Sundays in a row, April eleventh, April eighteenth, and April twenty-fifth, of the year 1778.

It was the same little church with the wooden steeple and vaulted roof in which the future bride had been christened. The ceiling was exceedingly curious—the keel of a wooden sailing ship turned upside down, crystal chandeliers suspended from it.

Yeyette listened, as if in a dream, to her name spoken aloud by the priest as he read the marriage proclamation: Marie-Josèphe-Rose, from now on to be known as *Rose,* the child's name of Yeyette to be dropped, as unsuitable for a young lady on the brink of matrimony . . . Although before she would get used to being called Rose, she would change her name again.

30

Part I

Gifts and congratulations poured in at La Pagerie Plantation: aunts and uncles, cousins and friends coming to offer their
good wishes. Rose blushed and bloomed under the rain of compliments. The center of attention was a lovely spot to be. She
could not help enjoying it, although her father shilly-shallied
about their departure date.

France and England were at war again, snatching and grab-
bing at each other's colonies in the New World. The English
fleet was threatening the French Antilles. It was certainly no
time to consider an Atlantic crossing. Furthermore, as a captain
in the island militia, Monsieur de Tascher's place was with
his regiment, standing off the British.

But Aunt Edmée had had enough of his excuses: "Alas,"
she wrote, "why can't I fly over there and get you? Come, come
now, hurry, hurry! . . . A young man's ardor may cool if he
is kept waiting too long."

War or no war, Rose and her father had to embark immediately.

In the late summer of 1779, he took advantage of a convoy
setting out from Fort-Royal for the French port of Brest, secur-
ing passage for himself, for Rose, and her maid, aboard the
partially armed royal vessel, the *Ile-de-France,* which, along
with several others, would make the voyage under the escort of
the French frigate, *Pomona,* bristling with cannon.

On the sailing day, the entire de Tascher family, including

the remotest cousins, accompanied the travelers to the dock, to the small skiff which would take them out to board their ship waiting in the harbor. Baron de Tascher, the Commander of the Port, Madame de Tascher de la Pagerie and Manette stayed on the shore, waving good-bye until the *Ile-de-France* was lost to sight.

Rose stood at the stern of the ship to wave her last farewells to her uncle, her mother, and her sister, to catch the last white flutter of their handkerchiefs.

When she put away her own handkerchief, she went to the port-side rail to try to catch a glimpse of Trois Ilets, across the bay, the three familiar dots marking her home shore.

Would she ever see any of them again? Either the islets or her family? She supposed she should be crying, and probably would have started there and then, had not the *Ile-de-France,* at that very moment, rounded the Virgin's Point—she had to put off the tears until she had had her first look into the open sea.

The best place for viewing the sea was at the prow of the ship, spanking against the waves, heading north. As soon as they cleared the northern-most tip of the island and entered the Martinique Passage, between Martinique and Dominica, they would be heading east, toward the Old World, toward Europe, toward France.

Even as she steadied herself against the wind that bellied the sails, and tried to get her balance on the heaving deck, Yeyette found that she still could not quite believe that it was really she, she herself, Marie-Josèphe-Rose—and not one of her two sisters —who was on her way to Paris, city of her dreams! On her way to a meeting with her romantic fiancé, on her way to the altar! Perhaps she should pinch herself to make sure she was not walking in her sleep? And perhaps she would have, had not the thought occurred to her that it would be very impertinent on her part to pinch a lady as distinguished as the future Viscountess de Beauharnais.

As the *Ile-de-France* entered the Martinique Passage, heading for the Atlantic Ocean, Rose was looking ahead into the endless blue of sky and sea and, beyond that, into her own future—a future more extraordinary, more fabulous than any she could have called up in her wildest flights of fancy. She was sailing off into as strange and splendid a destiny as any in recorded history.

PART
II

When the *Ile-de-France* limped into harbor on October 12, 1779, battered by storms, having escaped the English cannon, Monsieur de Tascher was so ill and weak that he had to be helped ashore. Rose was not a good sailor either, and probably spent most of that long, rough crossing on the bed in her dark and stuffy cabin. The cabins as well as the decks were drenched during the worst of the weather; this we know by the fact that even Monsieur de Tascher's important papers and documents, locked away in a metal chest, suffered water damage.

As soon as word reached Paris from the seaport, Aunt Edmée and her godson set off by carriage for Brest to greet the voyagers.

Alexandre could hardly wait to meet and to inspect his bride-to-be, though in recent months he had expressed some misgivings as this letter to his father shows: "We are not expected to go through with the marriage, are we, if we find one another repulsive?"

But on October 27, the meeting took place. Rose, unfortunately, left no letters, no diary to give us her first impression. Fortunately, Alexandre did, writing to his father in Paris: "Mademoiselle de la Pagerie may strike you as less pretty than might have been expected, but I can assure you that her delightful manner and the sweetness of her nature exceed our fondest expectations."

Though not the most enthusiastic reaction on the part of the groom, for Rose, on the other hand, it was apparently a case of love at first sight. She was swept off her feet by this dashing young officer in his white uniform trimmed with silver-gray, his sword at his side, his black, three-cornered hat set jauntily on his head, his exquisite, polished manners, and his air of gallantry and self-confidence. Older and more sophisticated women than little sixteen-year-old Rose had lost their hearts to this young dandy.

Unaware of Alexandre's disappointment, on December 13, 1779, Rose went trustingly and joyously into marriage with him.

Her trust and joy, her girlish delusions lasted little longer than the honeymoon. By April, Alexandre had left his bride to go off to a houseparty at the invitation of his socially prominent La Rochefoucauld cousins. His wife, he felt, was neither grand enough nor elegant enough for his grand and elegant friends at the magnificent Château de la Roche-Guyon. She had neither read the books nor seen the plays nor heard the concerts which Parisian society was talking about; their jokes about the Countess of Such-and-Such or the Duke of So-and-So would all be lost on her; she could never hold up her end in that sparkling, witty conversation. To Alexandre's way of thinking, his wife was a little ignoramus, frumpish in her island trousseau, and he would not take her along and take the chance of being embarrassed by her.

She was a Creole—a person of French or Spanish origin born in the islands or on the shores of the Caribbean—and the ignorance of the Creole ladies was a standing joke in France. "We were all acquainted with great ladies of that origin," one Paris gentleman wrote in his diary, "who, while taking their place in the highest society, scarcely knew how to read, much less to write." Alexandre was determined that his wife should be no laughingstock.

Alexandre was a snob with a highly exaggerated opinion of his own intelligence and knowledge, but there is no denying that Rose did lack a formal education. She could read and write, but that was all. She was, furthermore, a newcomer in a strange land—even her soft, slurred Creole accent was noticeable to French ears—and it would take time for her to adjust to a new world and a new society. Time to learn was what her husband denied her. It was in her favor that she was a good listener and, eventually, she profited by it, coming to be considered a delightful conversationalist. In time, she came to be an ornament of the society Alexandre frequented; during their marriage, he never gave her a chance. If he was not off visiting, that first year of their marriage, he was off somewhere in garrison with his regiment.

Neglected by her husband, Rose tried to console herself with her jewel case of Beauharnais heirlooms and her splendid Paris townhouse. But there were no parties to which to wear the diamonds and, with her father-in-law and her aunt as her only company, the house was as lonely as it was large.

"Do not poison the pleasure I take in your letters by reproaches," was her husband's reply to her tearful messages. "I am thrilled by your expression of a desire to improve yourself. To join a cultivated mind to your natural modesty will make an accomplished lady of you. If I could kiss you as I would like to, your plump little cheeks would glow and show it!"

Instead of making love to his wife, Alexandre was proposing to instruct her. To his former tutor he wrote: "I propose to make up for the sad neglect of the first fifteen years of her life by drawing up a plan for her education: lessons in geography and history, reading aloud of verse by our best poets, memorizing outstanding passages by our best dramatists."

There were to be lessons on the harp by Petrini, Paris's popular music master, while Alexandre himself would coach his wife in the art of letter writing—a skill in which she would have much practice, since he was so often away from home. Oddly enough, it was the subject in which Rose excelled. But even so, at sixteen, she would have preferred a husband at home, close by, to a professor, at long distance.

In December, after months of separation, Rose welcomed Alexandre back to Paris in time for their first wedding anniversary.

Then he was gone again, to rejoin his regiment, and she was alone for almost all the long months of her pregnancy, a condition she discovered soon after his departure.

Alexandre returned to the gay life of a bachelor; as he wrote his former tutor: "I thought at first that I could live happily with my wife, and pursued my plans for her education until I finally recognized an indifference and unwillingness to improve herself which convinced me that I was wasting my time. It was then that I reached the decision to abandon the education of my wife to anyone who cared to take it over. And so, instead of spending my time at home with a creature with whom I can find nothing in common, I have to a great extent resumed my bachelor life."

Alexandre showed no more patience as a teacher than as a husband: the honeymoon months, and the months of a first pregnancy can scarcely be considered the ideal time to start a bewildered young bride on a course of higher learning.

Not that Rose would ever be the truly studious type, but she had an excellent memory when she cared to exercise it, and, when a subject really interested her, she made herself proficient in it.

Alexandre put in one of his rare appearances in Paris on September 3, 1781, the birth date of their son, Eugene—a handsome baby, a no less handsome man, with portraits by all the great artists of the time to prove it.

But his father did not linger long in Paris. By November, he set out on a pleasure tour of Italy and stayed for months, not returning to his family until July of 1782.

In September, he left them again, this time without so much as a word of warning or a farewell embrace. He left his wife asleep, in the middle of the night, preferring to tell her by letter of his decision to sail for the New World, to join the French or the American forces in the war against the British. The American Revolution had broken out in 1775, and hundreds of Frenchmen sympathetic to the cause of the American colonies had sailed west to volunteer their services in the War for Independence. Alexandre was not only a late arrival, he saw no active duty; he seemed less eager to get into the fight than to loiter in Martinique checking into his wife's girlhood reputation.

If Rose had felt herself neglected during the first year of marriage, she considered herself abandoned in the second. She no longer troubled to reply to the occasional abusive letter from her faithless, wandering husband.

And in Paris, in April of 1783, the Beauharnais's second child, a girl, was born, and christened Hortense.

Alexandre was indignant that news of his daughter's birth should reach him, not first hand from his wife, but second or third hand through Rose's relatives on the island. He now turned on her viciously, accusing her of misconduct, and ordering her out of his house in Paris.

Women of the eighteenth century could not look to the law for protection of their rights, and the rights they did have were few. Both their persons and their property were, to a great extent, subject to the will—even the whim—of their fathers, brothers, or husbands.

Alexandre's own father stood up for Rose against her husband's slander, protested her innocence as a girl and as a wife, and tried to bring about a reconciliation, which only made Alexandre the angrier. He demanded that Rose be out of the house before he returned to Paris, that she take herself either back home to Martinique or to a convent. In one especially insulting letter, he forbade her so much as "a tear or a protest," and threatened to show himself "a tyrant" if she defied his orders.

Rose had no choice but to leave the house and go to a convent. Her two-year-old son could go with her, but she could not take her infant daughter, who had to be sent to a foster mother in the country.

The convent she chose, with Aunt Edmée's good counsel, was the most fashionable refuge in Paris, the Pentemont. It was a place of refuge for wives abandoned by their husbands or in process of separation, for sisters and daughters mistreated by brothers or fathers, for homeless orphans in search of husbands. The ladies of the best French society, in time of trouble, headed straight for the Pentemont.

As things turned out, it served Rose as a finishing school. There she came in contact with members of France's most prominent families. She was an attentive observer, and took note of their every word, every intonation, every expression of opinion, every custom, gesture, mannerism. With a good ear and an imitative tongue, she was soon speaking a pure Parisian French instead of her earlier Creole French. Eighteenth-century French society was famous for its air of elegance, its grand manner, which Rose soon made her own.

This pretty and wistful young woman of twenty with her winsome, golden haired little boy must have been an appealing figure. That "exceedingly sweet disposition" which her father had mentioned came to win her many lifelong friends. If her island trousseau had looked dowdy, she had by then—after four years in Paris—learned how to dress fashionably as well as becomingly. She had perfect taste, a flair for style, and a passion for clothes. By the time she arrived at the Pentemont, the awkward, adolescent stage was past . . . no more "plump cheeks" such as Alexandre had referred to in his letter; by then, she had become the slender, sleek and shapely, the exquisite and graceful creature who delights our eye today on canvas and in marble.

During this time, a lawyer was preparing Rose's plea for a legal separation from Alexandre. There was more than enough evidence to prove that he had completely failed her as a husband, that he had treated her harshly and inconsiderately, finally deserting her and their children. Alexandre's father was a witness to his daughter-in-law's blameless conduct, and at the end of a year of argument between attorneys, Alexandre agreed to a settlement out of court on the terms set by his wife; he even made a public admission that his accusations against her had been reckless and unfounded. Recognizing the justice of her charges of injury and neglect, he pledged himself to the payment of a substantial allowance for his wife's support and an additional amount for the maintenance of their daughter.

Their little son, Eugene, by the terms of the legal separation, was to remain with his mother until he reached the age of five; this age he reached in 1786, and was then turned over to his father for his education.

In 1788, Rose took five-year-old Hortense home with her to the West Indies. Rose's father and sister were both seriously ill, and Rose's mother longed to see her daughter and granddaughter.

Many years later Hortense wrote in her memoirs, "We set out alone, my Mother and I, from Le Havre, where violent winds almost overturned the ship, and we came close to perishing before we had cleared the harbor.

"Upon our arrival in Martinique," Hortense remembered, "we were joyously welcomed by our family. The quiet, peaceful life we led, visiting at one plantation, then at another, seemed to please my Mother, for we remained there nearly three years."

It may have been quiet and peaceful in far-off Martinique in 1789, but not in France. July fourteenth marked the fall of the Bastille, that grim, gray fortress-prison, symbol of royal tyranny and injustice, overwhelmed, battered down by a desperate and angry populace. The French Revolution, coming soon after the American Revolution, echoed many of the same battle cries: "Life, Liberty and the Pursuit of Happiness" was the Americans' expression for what they fought for; "Liberty, Equality and Fraternity" was how the French expressed similar aims.

The French had read what the Americans were writing

about the rights of man. In eighteenth-century France a man had no rights. The king held the power of life and death over his subjects. If the king said, "Off with his head," off it came; if the king said, "Off to the Bastille," off he went to be shut up there, perhaps for life, perhaps without ever knowing what the charges were against him, with no lawyer, no judge, no jury to appeal to.

Inequality was the basis of the entire French system; the social and political structure was like a pyramid: the king at the top; below him the lords of the nobility and of the church; at the very bottom of the heap—supporting and holding up all the rest, despised by and burdened down by them, paying all the national taxes and supplying all the labor—was the common man. He was the man without a title, the peasant, the farmer, the laborer, the craftsman, the shop-keeper—The People. In France in 1789, anger over the abuses of a thousand years suddenly boiled up. The people demanded representation in a national assembly and they demanded a constitution.

B y 1790, the winds of discontent had blown all the way to the West Indies: slaves, freedmen, mulattoes, and under-privileged whites rioted in Martinique on September seventh. Hortense tells how she and her mother escaped in the very nick of time: "The Revolution had begun in the colony. The governor urged us to flee at once. We were staying at Government House in Fort-Royal when suddenly, one evening, my mother was notified that the town was under attack. She rushed out at once to take refuge on a ship in the harbor. As we crossed the Savannah, a cannonball fell close beside us. The next day, the rioters overwhelmed the town, and ordered the royal French naval vessels to return to port, threatening them with fire from the fort. The crew of our ship shouted back that they were determined to return to France, and hurried to pull out of range of the shore battery. At that very moment, the cannon began to boom, but we escaped their shots. Fate had spared us."

Fate spared them again and again: in late October, after a stormy fifty-two day passage, the heavily armed frigate on which they sailed ran aground and almost capsized on the North African shore, just across from the Rock of Gibraltar. They barely managed to make it into Toulon harbor on October twenty-ninth.

Rose had learned, by newspaper and by mail, of the events that had rocked and shaken France during her two year absence. Even so, she was startled to see the red-white-and-blue revolutionary flags flying over the forts of Toulon harbor in place of the old white royal flag with its golden lilies or fleur-de-lis, the emblem of France's Bourbon kings. And she was taken aback to hear herself addressed as

Part II

"Citizeness," instead of "Madame" or "Viscountess." Those despised titles, symbolic of class distinctions, had been dropped after the Revolution.

On the road north from the coast to Paris, Rose caught frightening glimpses of flame and smoke—castles everywhere ablaze, under attack by peasants enraged at absentee landlords who had so long exploited and oppressed them.

Paris had become the center of government. Paris mobs had attacked the palace of Versailles and brought the king and queen back with them to the city. The National Assembly met in Paris and, in 1791 when the final draft of the Constitution was completed, it was Citizen Alexandre Beauharnais, Rose's husband, who was President of that body.

Alexandre was one of the noblemen who had cast his lot with the people and helped to lead the fight for liberty. His brother, on the other hand, had remained loyal to his class and king, and had fled from France to join the army being gathered by the Bourbon princes to attack France, to recover the nation from the revolutionaries and restore it to a monarchy. The other monarchs of Europe, fearful lest the germ of revolution spread from France to their kingdoms, were ready and willing to join the attack against the revolutionaries.

As these mighty armed forces invaded France in 1792, the reaction was violent: panic seized the nation. In August, the Tuileries Palace was stormed, and the royal family imprisoned.

In September, the first French Republic was proclaimed and, unfortunately, baptized in blood as Paris rioters dragged hundreds of priests and aristocrats from their prison cells and slaughtered them on the streets.

By this time most of Rose's friends had fled from France. She was terrified, and tried to send the children to safety in England, but her husband, as a good revolutionary, was indignant. He sent after them and had them brought back from the coast to Paris. He made no objection, however, when Rose insisted on taking them to live in the suburbs, in the pretty and quiet village of Croissy, on the Seine, ten miles up the river from the capital.

As a leader in the revolutionary councils, Alexandre insisted that his children be brought up not as aristocrats, but as good little republicans, and that meant learning a trade: Eugene was sent as an apprentice to a cabinet-maker; Hortense was sent to a seamstress.

Rose was grateful to be out of ear-shot of the hideous din on January 21, 1793, when King Louis XVI was driven in a cart through howling, jeering mobs to the Place of the Revolution, to the guillotine—the newest instrument of execution, whose sharp blade slid swiftly and surely, straight down from the top of a wooden frame to slice off the neck of the victim.

Rose shuddered at the news of the King's trial and execution; she could not forget that her own father had served the

King's mother as a page. Her father had been at Versailles the very day this ill-fated king had been born!

By the summer of 1793, Alexandre had been promoted to the rank of general and made commander of the French Army of the Rhine, defending the northeastern frontier of the Republic against attack by the combined royalist forces streaming in from the German states. But General Beauharnais failed to give a good account of himself, and was soon relieved of his command. Shortly after that, he was arrested and sent to the Carmes Prison in Paris: as good a revolutionary as he had been, he was under suspicion as a member, by birth, of the detested nobility. Every aristocrat, no matter what his record, was considered a natural enemy of the people, a traitor to the Republic.

Rose, as the wife of an accused traitor, as a former aristocrat herself, was bound to come under suspicion, too. One needed to do no more, in those days, than to point the finger of suspicion to bring about an arrest. Someone pointed it at Rose—she never discovered who; her arrest came in the middle of the night of April 22, 1794.

"Don't wake the children," Hortense quotes her mother as whispering to their governess. "I could not bear their tears. I could not tear myself from their arms."

"Our awakening," Hortense concludes, "was cruel . . . suddenly alone, deprived . . . of both mother and father."

By an odd coincidence, Rose was taken to the Carmes, the

same prison to which her husband had been sent months earlier. It was the most horrible of the many horrible revolutionary prisons in Paris: old, dark, damp, its walls dripping with moisture and still blood-smeared from the September massacres of 1792. There were no windows, only barred slits in the thick stone walls; there were open latrines in the narrow corridors. The cells were crawling with rats, mice, and vermin; they were packed and jammed with over seven hundred miserable prisoners in that spring of 1794 when Rose arrived.

Living in such misery and under the constant threat of death, the aristocrats of France gave proof of a courage such as has rarely been seen before or since. Courage, good manners, and good humor were all part of their social code, and they preserved these to the end; under the most trying, most cruel conditions, morale stayed high in the dreadful revolutionary prisons.

Rose and her husband met occasionally in the prison courtyard and conferred politely, if aloofly, on the subject of the children. They wrote joint letters to Eugene and Hortense. Rose's were tender and affectionate: "My dear little Hortense, it hurts me to be separated from you and my dear Eugene. I never stop thinking of my two darling little children, whom I love and embrace with all my heart."

Alexandre's messages were stiff and formal; he always sounded more like a professor than a parent: "The best way to convince us that you miss and remember us is by assuring us that you are putting your time to good purpose and working hard."

When the prison authorities put an end to correspondence with the outside world, the children began writing out, in their own hand, the lists of food and clothing in the packages which they delivered each week to the prison gate. "Each of us, in turn," as Hortense explains the trick, "copied out the list so that, at least, our parents would know we were still alive."

A still cleverer trick of the children's was to write a note on a scrap of paper and fasten it under the collar of their mother's little dog, Fortuné. Fortuné was a fawn-colored pug with a black mask and a corkscrew of a tail; the dog could dart past the guard in a flash, find its way to its mistress's cell, then back to the children with her reply.

Once, during those long months, through some mysterious and unidentified person, Hortense and Eugene were given a glimpse of their prisoner parents. "An unknown lady came one day," as Hortense later wrote in the story of her life, "and mysteriously led us to the rear of a garden on a street near the prison, and up the stairs of a gardener's house, all the while cautioning us to the strictest silence. Across from us we could see a huge building . . . and then a window opening, in which my mother and father appeared. In surprise and great emotion, I stretched out my arms to them and cried out. They made signs to me to be still, but a guard at the foot of the prison wall had heard us, and began to shout. The unknown lady hurried us out, and home. . . . We learned later that the window of the prison had been sealed up. This was the last time I saw my father. A few days later he was dead."

This incident, a nightmare to haunt all Hortense's childhood, must have taken place in mid-July, for on the twenty-second of that month, her father's name was called out by the jailor at the Carmes Prison—he was one of the fifty or more prisoners to be transferred that day to the Conciergerie Prison, where the meetings of the Revolutionary Court were held.

There was never any doubt as to what the sentence of that court would be: the sentence would be death—it always was—with the execution taking place no later than the following day. Between the middle of June and the end of July, in that year of 1794, one thousand three hundred and sixty-seven heads fell in Paris alone, not to mention the thousands in the other cities and towns of the nation. For this was the period of "The Great Terror," as it has since come to be called in historic accounts of the Revolution. As fast as the death sentences emptied the prisons, new arrest-warrants filled them up again. A man named Robespierre had seized control of the government, and he used terror, deliberately, as a weapon, to wipe out all opposition, to retain his power, to turn the Revolution to the purposes he considered best for the nation.

When Alexandre Beauharnais's death sentence was pronounced on July twenty-second, he faced it as coolly and coura-
geously as did most of his fellow aristocrats, writing to his wife:
"My tender affection for our dear children and the brotherly
attachment which binds me to you can leave no doubt of the
sentiment with which I depart this life."

Rose trembled with fear that her name would follow her
husband's on the roll call of death announced daily by the jailor.
From day to day she sat shuddering, in panic, waiting in her
cell to be taken away.

Later, she told the story of those suspenseful hours to a
young friend named Georgette Ducrest, who recorded the story
in her memoirs, in Rose's own words:

*One morning, the jailor came into the cell where I slept with
the Duchess of Aiguillon and two other ladies. He told me that
he had come to take away my bed to give it to another prisoner.*

*"Does that mean that Madame Beauharnais is to have a bet-
ter bed?" the Duchess demanded sharply.*

*"It means that she won't be needing a bed of any kind," he
answered with a horrid grin. "It means that they are coming
to take her to the Conciergerie and from there to the guillotine."*

At these words my cell mates let out piercing shrieks.

56

Finally, to stop their weeping, I told them that they need not become so upset, that not only I would not be put to death, I would live to become the queen of France, as had once been predicted to me!

"Then why not begin making out the list of your Ladies of the Palace?" the Duchess inquired sarcastically.

"Ah, you are right, I hadn't thought of that. Very well, my dear, I'll begin by naming you my Lady of Honor, I promise you the appointment."

At which, these ladies' tears began to flow the faster; they were afraid I had gone out of my mind, stark raving mad! Actually, I was not putting on a show of courage. I was at that moment convinced that the prediction made to me by the fortune-teller in Martinique would come true!

When the Duchess seemed about to faint, Rose pulled her toward the window of the cell and opened it to give her friend a breath of air. That was when they saw a woman outside the prison walls making the strangest kind of gestures to attract their attention: first, she would point to her dress—"robe," in French; then she would pick up a stone—"pierre," in French. Finally, as Rose later told the story to Mademoiselle Ducrest, she began to understand the charade, to put the two words together: Robe–Pierre. The woman was trying to tell them something about Robespierre—Robe-s-Pierre! Next, the woman went through the motions of slitting her throat. What could that mean? Could it mean that Robespierre had been guillotined? Yes, it did. That was exactly what had happened. The bloody tyrant had at last been overthrown and executed! The Terror was at an end!

Rose and her cellmates joyously spread the word up and down the prison corridors. As Mademoiselle Ducrest reports Rose saying:

They brought me back my bed of leather-stripped webbing, on which I slept the soundest night's sleep of my life. Before I retired, I said to my friends: "You see, I have not been guillotined . . . and I shall yet be crowned queen of France!"

It made a very good story, and Mademoiselle Ducrest probably wrote it down just as it was told to her.

But it is doubtful that at the time Rose put much faith in her own prediction.

When she was released from prison early in August, she rushed home to Hortense and Eugene. The Terror was over, and she wanted to try to pick up the broken pieces of her life. But she found herself in a world she scarcely recognized, a world in upheaval—a Republic replacing an ancient monarchy, the old social and political order swept away—and she was unsure how she would provide for herself and the children. All the Beauharnais properties had been confiscated by the government. The only financial aid she could hope for would have to come from her parents in Martinique. However, relief from that quarter was uncertain in time of war, for English gunboats preyed on French cargo vessels bringing sugar and other supplies and aid from America to Europe.

What would become of Rose and the children? What did the future hold for them? What about the prediction made by the fortune-teller, twenty-some years ago, in the tumble-down shack near Trois Ilets? What the old slave-woman had said was that Rose's future held "both good and bad . . . some happy things, some unhappy. . . . The unhappy things, first."

The unhappy things had happened just as Euphémie had said they would: "You will sail across the seas to marry and have children," and so she had. "But that marriage will end in sorrow, with your husband's death," and so it had. "A terrible death"—none could have been more terrible, Alexandre's bloody, severed head bouncing on the scaffold of the guillotine. "A death such as no one had died before"—the guillotine was used for the first time during the Revolution. Rose had been "left a widow" and her "children fatherless"—just as Euphémie had foretold it, so it had come to pass.

The first part of the prediction had come true. What about the second part? The part about Rose's becoming queen of France? That part was still absurd, ridiculous, nonsensical. Rose could not believe it, but she could not disbelieve it, either.

The world had been turned upside down, all the rules had been changed with the Revolution; almost anything could happen, these days. Marie Antoinette was no longer queen, her execution having taken place in 1793, less than a year after the King's.

But how did that bring Rose any closer to the throne of France or of any other country?

Only a king could make her a queen, and there were no kings in sight, no kings nor even princes waiting on her door-step . . . only a shabby, down-at-the-heels little general.

PART
III

This little general—no taller than Rose, if as tall—talked big, about his victories to come, about his Lucky Star and his Destiny, but most people laughed at him in his old boots with their worn-down heels and his faded overcoat with powder burns on the sleeve.

No one really knew much about him except that, in 1793, he had turned the big guns of the fort at Toulon on the combined English and Spanish fleets, running them out of that important French seaport as no one else had been able to do. And this stunning artillery strategy had won him a promotion to the rank of brigadier general, at age twenty-four.

He was born in Corsica in 1769, little more than a year after that island became a French possession. By only a narrow margin of time was Napoleone Buonaparte born a Frenchman; later he would drop the *e* off the end of his first name and the *u* out of the middle of his last name, to Frenchify it. The Bonapartes were of Italian descent, having moved to Corsica from the mainland some two hundred years earlier. Napoleon was the second oldest of a family of eight children, a typical Corsican family: close, devoted, fiercely loyal to one another even when they fought like wildcats, as they would later do over the treasure, territories, crowns, and titles of their brother Napoleon's conquests.

Their father, as judge in the courts of Corsica, was entitled to send his sons to France on scholarships furnished by the king to sons of noblemen and government officials. At the age of nine, in 1778, Napoleon was sent to France to learn the language, and the next year, he was enrolled in the Royal Military Academy to begin his five-year course of training. As early as that, he knew that the army was to be his career.

He was a lonely boy, made to feel an outsider with his peculiar name, his rasping Corsican-Italian accent and his crude island manners, a poor bumpkin from the provinces among the sons of wealthy French aristocrats. He was marked as a foreigner among Frenchmen, as he would always be—even as Emperor of the French, even as France's most fabulous hero.

Left to himself, he concentrated on his studies—especially history, geography, and mathematics—doing so well on his final examination that he was awarded another scholarship, to the Military College in Paris, from which he was graduated in 1785 with the rank of second- or sub-lieutenant; by 1792, he had reached the rank of captain. In December of 1793 came his first victory at Toulon and his generalship.

But when he was assigned by the War Department to an infantry brigade in the west, he balked. He refused to abandon his beloved artillery, and he was reluctant to become embroiled in the civil war raging in the province of La Vendée, where the French peasants loyal to the local noblemen and priests were up in arms against the French republican forces.

In 1795, without a command and without pay, General Bonaparte polished his worn boots, tightened his belt, and studied the map of Italy where he thought France's archenemy, Austria, should be met one day and tackled. Stubborn and recalcitrant he might have been, but his proposals for a campaign strategy were so interesting that they were taken under consideration by the War Department.

"All that I am waiting for is a chance to take part in a battle," he wrote to his brother Joseph, about this time, "to snatch the crown of victory from the hands of Fortune or to die on the field of glory."

Genereal Bonaparte was certainly the skinniest and most extraordinary creature I had ever seen in my life," one young woman who met him in Paris during those lean and hungry years would later say. "In accordance with the fashions of the day, his hair hung down in 'dogs ears' so long as to brush his shoulders. . . . All that hair looked especially strange in contrast to his extraordinary eyes . . . magnificent eyes that lighted up when he talked. . . . When he talked about the siege of Toulon, he held our interest . . . and his face became very animated." He had "very fine features," she declared, "his mouth was especially well formed. All he needed to be considered handsome was to have been better dressed." He struck her as "a fiery man—a man of spirit," but somehow it struck her, too, that "he was a man one would not care to come across in a lonely wood at night." Above all, he impressed her as "a man who laughed at danger."

That too was how he impressed the leaders of the National Convention—the governing body of the nation—who asked him to defend the Republic against a sudden royalist plot to regain control from the people and set up a monarchy again.

General Bonaparte had forty cannon drawn up in front of the Tuileries Palace in Paris, early on the morning of October 5th, 1795, felled the first two hundred attackers, and turned back a force of twenty thousand, five times the strength of his own men.

Shortly afterward a *Directoire,* a special committee of five members, was set up to administer the affairs of the nation, and its first move was to appoint its protector, young General Bonaparte, to the top military post, commander of the Army of the Interior.

His first move was to prevent another uprising. He ordered that all arms, all weapons, all guns, all swords, in the hands of private citizens, be turned in immediately at military headquarters.

Fourteen-year-old Eugene Beauharnais "rebelled at the thought of turning in his dead father's sword," as his sister Hortense tells the story, "and rushing to headquarters, asked to speak with the General. He said he would rather be killed than to give up so precious a relic. The boy expressed himself so warmly and so well that the General was touched and granted his request to keep the weapon, adding that he would like to meet the woman who had inspired such noble sentiments in her son."

Shortly after, he went to pay his respects to the boy's mother.

And that, according to Hortense, was how the meeting came about between General Bonaparte and the widow Beauharnais. Since Napoleon told much the same story, years later, to one of his biographers, there is no reason to doubt that this is exactly how it happened.

To the same biographer, Napoleon said that, at his very first meeting with the lady, he had been struck by "her extraordinary grace and irresistibly sweet manner." From that time on, he was to be seen constantly at her doorstep. He attended her weekly receptions where he was honored to meet the most distinguished society of the capital. He became Madame Beauharnais's regular escort at the Opera, at the theatre, at government functions in the Luxembourg Palace; he entertained her at dinner at his luxurious new headquarters, drove her around the city and the countryside in his fine new carriage. They even exchanged portraits.

And he changed her name from Rose to Josephine. Just why, it is not clear. Maybe because he was insanely jealous, and did not want to call her by the name her husband or earlier admirers had called her—she became his own, very own, Josephine. He may have chosen the name because there was already a Josèphe in her baptismal name, Marie-Josèphe-Rose. Or maybe because the name of his older brother, Joseph, was dear to him. Whatever the reason, Rose became Josephine to him—and so, to the history books.

Young Eugene had played cupid in this romance, but Hortense took a dislike to the General when she met him. He teased her and tweaked her ear—his tweaks, pinches, love-pats were signs of affection on his part, but even his bravest officers winced in pain at them! He frightened Hortense, and she feared that he would be very strict with her and Eugene.

"When he came to my mother's house to visit he could not but notice what a chilly reception we gave him," Hortense wrote in her *Memoirs*. "He made an effort to win us over, but had no success with me. Every time I came home to Paris"— both Hortense and Eugene had been sent away to boarding school—"I found him there, more and more attentive to my mother. I broke into tears, begging her not to re-marry; above

70

all, not a man whose career was likely to take her far away from us. . . . But the General already had more influence over her than I did. Even so, I think that my opposition to the marriage caused her to put off her decision. . . . If she re-marries, I said to my brother with whom I shared my fears, *Maman* will not love us as much."

Maman did put off her decision; she could not make up her mind as to how she felt about her "little general," as she referred to him in her letters. Writing to a friend she said: "I am being urged to re-marry. You have met General Bonaparte at my house. Well then, it is he who wishes to serve as father to the orphans of Alexandre Beauharnais, as husband to his widow. Do I love him? you are going to ask me. Well, no. But, worse still, I find myself in a state of indifference, lukewarmness which disturbs me."

In the beginning, it is clear, Napoleon was head over heels in love with Josephine, not she with him. Before it was all over, however, things would change.

At that point, Napoleon was no great catch, being the mainstay of a large and demanding family. His father had died, and Napoleon had brought them all—his mother, his younger sisters, and brothers—from Corsica to France. Josephine's friends and legal adviser warned her against marriage with a penniless army man on the very first rung of the shaky military ladder. An adventurer who was younger than herself, who might well be killed in action and leave her with still more children to bring up . . . and still without financial security. As her notary said, the general might be an excellent officer, but he had "nothing at this point to recommend him except his cape and his sword!"

Somehow, the General convinced her that his sword was enough: "My sword is at my side," she quotes him as saying, "and with that, I shall go far."

"I don't know why," Josephine wrote to her friend, "but sometimes this absurd self-confidence of his impresses me to the point of believing anything possible to this singular man— anything at all that might come into his head to undertake! And with that fantastic imagination of his, who can guess what he might undertake?"

He was about to embark on the campaign in Italy. The *Directoire* had assigned him, in early 1796, to that command, a risky task at which many another French general had failed. He was ready to leave Paris to join his army in the south of France. Josephine was finally forced to make up her mind, one way or the other.

She was a widow with expensive tastes and with two children to support and educate—all on the most irregular kind of income: whatever small amounts her family could spare to send to her from Martinique. Her mirror assured her that she was still lovely to look at, at age thirty-two, but how much longer could she count on that? Many a gentleman was dancing attendance upon her, but none was offering marriage. In a world turned topsy-turvy, she was alone and frightened. She could not waver longer. She would gamble on her general.

"My mother's resistance ended when she saw General Bonaparte on the verge of departure," relates Hortense, who at the time was at a very select and fashionable school whose headmistress, Madame Campan, had been a lady-in-waiting to the late Queen Marie Antoinette, and who taught her pupils the elegant manners and deportment practiced at the court of Versailles. Later, that training would come in very handy for Hortense. "It fell to Madame Campan to break the news [of Josephine's decision to marry] to Eugene and me," Hortense continues. "Our mother lacked the courage, knowing what distress it would cause us. I was, it is true, very sadly affected, but Madame Campan tried to calm me by pointing out the advantages for my brother. He was eager for a military career and could not begin it under better auspices than those of the general who was to be his stepfather."

On February twenty-eighth, the wedding bans were published. On March second, General Bonaparte's appointment to the command of the Army of Italy was publicly announced. On March eighth, the wedding contract was signed—the bride subtracting four years from her age, the groom gallantly adding eighteen months to his, to minimize the difference and make them both a congenial twenty-eight.

On March ninth, the wedding took place in the office of the Mayor of the Second District of Paris. Not one of the seven members of the Bonaparte family had been notified, much less invited. The groom waited until after the wedding to ask his mother and his older brother for their formal consent, though he should have done so beforehand, according to the strict Corsican tribal customs.

Nor had Josephine been willing to risk her children's sulks or tears. The difference was that the Beauharnais children would become reconciled and devoted to the groom, whereas the Bonapartes never would, to the bride.

The bride appeared at her wedding with two friends and a trusted legal adviser, promptly at the appointed hour of eight, looking glamorous in one of her sheer, filmy, clinging tunics, and with a golden bandeau circling her chestnut curls.

Only the groom was missing.

From eight to ten, Josephine practiced patience, which she was to need in order to live with a man so preoccupied as to lose track of time on his wedding night!

As the clock struck ten, the clack of boots and the clank of swords on the stone entry steps roused the Mayor from a cat nap behind his desk. Within a matter of minutes after the ar-

74

rival of General Bonaparte and his aide-de-camp, the golden wedding band had been slipped on the bride's finger—a ring engraved "To Destiny,"—which would be worn as a talisman on the finger of Josephine's grandson when he entered Paris as Emperor Napoleon III in 1851. Before ten-thirty had chimed, the brief civil ceremony had been concluded, congratulations had been offered, and the newlyweds in their carriage were en route back to the bride's house on the rue Chantereine for a thirty-six-hour honeymoon.

Josephine's children were not at home, but Fortuné, the little pug dog with the corkscrew tail, growled ferociously at the strange man across the counterpane. The children would finally make friends with Napoleon, but Fortuné never would, and left teeth marks on the General's leg to prove it.

On March eleventh, General Bonaparte came to what he called "the cruel parting" from his Josephine; his orders tore him away from her, and he drove out of Paris in his carriage, at his usual breakneck speed. He was off on the greatest military adventure of any the world had seen since that of Alexander, that of Caesar—his two personal heroes.

He was on his way to join the poorly equipped, poorly trained, ragtag French army, waiting for him at Nice on the Mediterranean. Within weeks, he made that young, ragged band of raw recruits into one of the great fighting forces of all time.

He piled victory upon victory in the months to come. People talked about miracles, but Napoleon's success was the result of military genius and personal heroism. The little general studied his maps and the Italian terrain; he worked out a masterful plan of attack and surprise, and led his men into the thick of battle, sword in one hand, flag in the other.

But despite the pace of his life and his success, he did not neglect his Josephine. He wrote daily, nightly, or twice in every twenty-four hours, or even more often, though some letters, he told her, were "too foolish to send," and so he just stuffed them in his pockets. He scrawled out these messages to her in his tent, at his camp table, upon his map-box, by the light of camp-fires across all of Italy. His letters are almost illegible—his handwriting terrible, at its best—they are ink-spattered and splotched, blots and blobs of ink where his pen raced and sput-tered. They were then sent off, on the gallop, by special messen-ger, his trusted courier, Moustache, and delivered as swiftly to Josephine in her little house on the rue Chantereine in Paris as were the military dispatches to the five Directors in the Luxem-bourg Palace. These letters are full of battle names and his "thousand and one kisses" for his sweetheart. They ring with love and passion for his "beautiful and enchanting," his "sweet and gentle," his "tender and kind," his "Incomparable

Josephine!" So romantic, one might almost think them from the pen of a poet instead of a tough and alert military man.

Josephine thought this all rather "funny," which was the word she used. "He's funny—Bonaparte!" she said, smiling, to a friend of hers, as she read him some of her husband's impassioned personal messages. She seemed flattered, in a way, to have inspired such great love in a man fast becoming famous across the continent of Europe, but she seemed a little embarrassed by it, too . . . as if now that they were married and settled, they were too old for such romantic antics.

Josephine enjoyed her husband's Italian triumphs. She enjoyed the acclaim as the wife of the new national hero: in his name, she accepted all the tributes, stood in the place of honor at the victory celebrations which followed one upon another. The name of the street where she lived was officially changed to the rue de la Victoire, Victory Street, and she was hailed everywhere as "Notre Dame des Victoires," Our Lady of Victory.

Somehow, in the minds of the French people and the French army, she came to be associated with Napoleon's destiny, his lucky star; she was part of its shining light. He, himself, felt that this was true: did not his triumphs date from his marriage with her? Why should she discourage (what woman would not enjoy) so flattering an association?

Josephine wanted to go on being a celebrity, but she wanted to do so in Paris. She did not want to leave that gay social whirl to go to Italy to join her hero-husband on a honeymoon, as he was urging her to do.

Hortense, who wanted her mother to go down in history as a noble figure, tried but failed to do away with all the letters Napoleon wrote to his wife at this time, imploring her to come to him, at least to write to him. "If you loved me, you would write to me at least twice daily!" he reproached her in one letter that escaped Hortense's bonfires.

Josephine feared to go into a theater-of-war, so her husband rushed to make it safe for her to come to Milan, the key city of the campaign, which had fallen under his assault. His conquest of Piedmont opened up the passes through the Alps, the short-cut to France, the speediest route for reinforcements, for supplies, for Josephine. By the summer of 1796, the French government declared it safe for her to travel, and she could put it off no longer.

On July thirteenth, the conqueror of Italy reaped his reward: Josephine rode into Milan, into Napoleon's open arms. He welcomed her to the magnificent Serbelloni Palace which he had commandeered as their residence—"a pile of pinkish, crystal-flecked granite that sparkled like sugar-candy in the sun," as one visitor saw it.

"Once re-united with his wife at Milan," Napoleon's close friend and fellow-officer General Marmont wrote, "General Bonaparte was supremely happy, for he lived then for her and for her alone—a love so true, so pure, so exclusive had never possessed the heart of a man before, certainly not a man so outstanding and so superior as this one."

He could not bear to let her out of his sight for the rest of the campaign. He would rush out to battle and then back to her again. It was as if he drew from her the inspiration for his startling and original maneuvers. But once he let her come too close to the front lines: her carriage came under fire from an Austrian patrol boat on Lake Garda; two of the horses fell dead between the traces and one of the escort of soldiers tumbled dead out of his saddle. Josephine, her maid, and traveling companions, had to be taken out of the land-side door of the carriage, had to crawl on hands and knees to a ditch out of range of the guns, and had to travel on from there in a peasant cart.

She knew that her husband-general would fight through the Austrian encirclement that night to rescue her, and he did. The Austrian general, he promised her, "will pay dearly for your tears." And the Austrian general did. But Napoleon was contrite—his wife was right, he had been selfish, a battle zone was no place for a woman.

The Palace of Mombello, set deep within its large and beautiful park, eight miles from Milan, was a safe and delightful spot to spend the summer, a refreshing change from city life at the Serbelloni Palace.

Here the entire Bonaparte clan came to visit and to inspect

the bride. Of the five brothers, Joseph was the oldest, then came Napoleon, Lucien, Louis, and Jerome, the baby of the family, just thirteen that summer of 1797. Of the three girls, Elisa was the first born, the least attractive; next Pauline, the great beauty of the family, the great beauty of the age, and Napoleon's favorite; last was Caroline, future Queen of Naples, pretty, too, with her golden curls, blue eyes, and luscious complexion, "like white satin seen through rose-colored glasses," as one friend described her.

They rebuffed all of Josephine's gestures of friendship, but she kept on trying. She simply could not believe that, in time, her good will and warmth would not dispel the cold, spiteful glare from those piercing, jetty, Bonaparte eyes. But she was wrong, they were her mortal enemies, and would never relent until they had brought her down. They were greedy and jealous; she was in their way, she stood between them and their brother and the stream of gold that would flow in the wake of his conquests. They whispered that she was too old for her husband, too old to bear him children and, by Corsican standards, the success of a marriage was to be judged by the number of children it produced.

Napoleon's mother, tall and ramrod stiff with dignity and pride, did not take to this daughter-in-law with her elaborate wardrobe, her sophisticated air, her worldly charm, her elegant French manner. *Madame Mère*—Madam Mother, as Napoleon's mother would later be called—lacked all the social graces and so was suspicious of Josephine who had them all. Had her consent been asked by her son, as it should have been, she would never have approved this social butterfly, this fashion model, this flighty, wildly extravagant, frivolous, flirtatious, thirty-four-year-old Frenchwoman.

Surrounded by that horde of hostile Bonapartes, what a joy it was for Josephine to welcome her own dear son, Eugene, to Italy. At sixteen, he had been summoned from his school in France to begin his military training under his celebrated step-father.

A fine boy, he was developing into a fine man, genuinely genial, kind, gay of heart, courageous, loyal, honorable—the only truly normal, well-adjusted member of the whole Beau-harnais-Bonaparte congregation, the best of the lot.

Antoine Gros, Josephine's favorite artist at that time, was commissioned to paint a portrait of handsome young Eugene in uniform, with his high-plumed hat and his aide-de-camp's in-signia: the white, fringed scarf, puffed and knotted just above the elbow.

Already a knowledgeable patroness of the arts, Josephine had brought young Gros from Genoa to Milan to paint a por-trait of Napoleon as the hero of the Arcole victory—flag in hand, leading the famous bloody charge across the bloody bridge. The only way Josephine could get him to hold still for the artist, as Gros later described the sittings to his mother, was to pull the hero, flag and all, into the chair beside her or onto her lap, holding him with embraces he did not care to break.

The hero's work in Italy was nearly done. The Pope had asked for peace early in the year, as had most of the Italian dukes and princes, and they soon discovered, to their sorrow, that the young French general was as skilled and ruthless a diplomat as he was a warrior.

By mid-summer of 1797, the Austrians were ready to talk peace too, and a treaty highly favorable to the young French Republic was negotiated by young General Bonaparte. He and his country were coming up in the world.

The French army's ammunition carts returned home loaded down with the prizes of war: gold and art, paintings and statuary from Italian palaces and churches which would eventually adorn the Museum of the Louvre which Napoleon would establish.

The Pope, to express his gratitude to General Bonaparte for sparing Rome from attack and occupation, presented the General's wife with a gift of pearls as large as pigeons' eggs. The other Italian potentates followed suit. It was the beginning of a collection of jewels more fabulous than any described in the tales of the *Arabian Nights*. Later, Josephine would have at her disposal all of the crown jewels of France—all the jewels collected throughout the centuries by former monarchs—but for her they were never enough. Josephine loved diamonds even better than did Marie Antoinette, who was known as the Queen of Diamonds. Napoleon could dictate to popes and kings and princes, but he could not control his wife's extravagances. Each year found her sending stones to be reset, rings to be made over into pins and pins into bracelets, ordering new mountings for old, exchanging rubies for emeralds or diamonds for pearls, and incurring considerable expense in each transaction. Throughout her years as empress, a shimmering stream of precious stones passed endlessly through her fingers.

Josephine crossed the Alps on her way back to Paris clutching her bulging jewel case. But en route home she made a detour; she wanted to see Venice.

Venice wanted to see her too: "One hundred and fifty thousand Venetians lined the canals to get a glimpse of her," wrote General Marmont, who was there. "The canals alive with song and fireworks throughout the night, every palazzo and every building illuminated, reflecting in the waters—a sea of flame; a glittering ball in the Doges' Palace, all the theatres open, the torches flaring until sunrise on the Piazza San Marco . . . the most brilliant, the gayest, the most splendorous entertainments" were offered to the General's lady. The General was pleased at the honors paid her, but displeased that she should be enjoying herself so light-heartedly without him. His brothers and sisters carried back to him tales of the attentions paid her by princes, dukes, and officers, tales about flirtations. Corsicans have a reputation for being jealous husbands and Napoleon lived up to the reputation.

Reaching Paris early in December, 1797, Napoleon paced the floor, impatient for his wife's arrival.

"All Paris rang with his name," as Hortense remembered, "and thronged in such great numbers to see The Conqueror of Italy that the sentries posted at the gateway to the house on Victory Street could scarcely deal with the crowds which fought for a chance to see him."

One of the few visitors permitted past the gates by the sentries was young Hortense, escorted by her grandfather Beauharnais to greet her stepfather Bonaparte. "What a change in our little house!" she was to write. "Formerly so quiet, it was filled now with generals and officers. At last, despite the crowds, we reached the General, who was surrounded by his staff. He gave me the fond and tender welcome of a father, telling me that my brother had been sent to Corfu and to Rome to bear the news of peace."

The General was very fond of Hortense, and always would be. At fourteen, she was the star pupil of her school, and the most popular. She was gay and animated, warm and outgoing, a joy to friends and family.

On January 2, 1798, she greeted her mother with total delight at their reunion after a year and a half's separation.

But Josephine had some stormy scenes to play with her jealous husband. She finally managed to convince him, however, that she had given him no cause for jealousy. She was so gentle and sweet, so tender, so pretty and enchanting, and he was still so much in love with her that he preferred to take her word instead of that of his family.

Besides, he was back at his maps again. They covered the floor of his study.

This time they were maps of Egypt. His next great military adventure was to be across the Mediterranean, in the East, a land that exercised a spell over him, where Alexander and Caesar had marched before him. "This little Europe cannot provide enough of glory," he told his secretary, Louis-Antoine-Bourrienne, the only friend he had made at the military academy.

General Bonaparte had persuaded the Directors to undertake an attack on Egypt instead of an invasion of England. He had calculated the risks on both and found that the odds favored the former. Napoleon proposed to cut England's commercial lifeline, her trade route to the East, to India; he proposed to take the province of Egypt from the Ottoman-Turkish

Empire and to make a French colony of it. The borders of France had been extended and secured by recent victories in Italy and Austria, and she was threatened by no enemy.

The Directors agreed to Napoleon's plan. They were growing somewhat nervous about this new strong man, this favorite of the people, and considered it worthwhile to risk a large expeditionary force to get the hero out of the country.

For all the blood and treasure spilled and spent on the Egyptian expedition of 1798–9, the net results in terms of territorial, economic, or diplomatic advantage to France proved to be absolutely zero. But, for once, a foolish war served a good purpose. It so happened that General Bonaparte took along scholars as well as soldiers, a one hundred and sixty-seven-member Commission of Arts and Sciences: engineers, mathematicians, chemists, botanists, zoologists, physicians, pharmacists, mapmakers, Orientalists, Arabists, antiquarians, artists, historians—to study, to explore, to describe, to map and to sketch, for the first time, the land of the Pharaohs, its tombs and monuments, its flora and fauna, its great River Nile. When Napoleon's scholars published their twenty-four volume *Description of Egypt,* in 1809, the science of Egyptology was born. When Napoleon's archaeologists discovered the Rosetta Stone, it proved to be the key whereby Egyptian hieroglyphics—until then, a mystery—could be deciphered.

Part III

The whole French fleet was called in to convoy the thirty thousand troops, and the mighty armada lay fully assembled and tugging at anchor in Toulon harbor when General and Madame Bonaparte, accompanied by Eugene, proudly attired in his aide-de-camp's uniform, drove into that seaport in early May of 1798.

Not until the very last moment was it decided that Josephine was not to accompany her husband. He had not wanted to be separated from her, he was still desperately in love: "His attachment to her bordered on idolatry," his secretary remarked at the time.

It was not true, as the malicious Bonapartes claimed, that their brother's wife had refused to go along, that it was she who had made the decision to remain in France—to continue her round of pleasures, the Bonapartes insinuated, in society and in the company of other men.

The reason for her not sailing with the expedition was that Napoleon was "fearful of an encounter with the English fleet," Josephine wrote to a friend from Toulon, "and did not want to expose me to the risk of that crossing."

As it happened, Napoleon's lucky star must have been shining brightly throughout that dangerous six weeks' crossing of the Mediterranean. Admiral Nelson and the British fleet gave constant chase, but never could quite catch up.

It was agreed that Josephine was to follow within two

87

months, when the sea might be safer. Besides, it would give her time first "to take the waters" at Plombières, as Napoleon urged her to do, to drink them and to bathe in them. The Europeans have always had—still have—great faith in the power of their mineral waters to heal and to cure various physical disabilities. Certain mineral springs are famous for their benefit to the liver, others to the kidneys, the spleen, or the stomach, or for rheumatic or arthritic aches and pains. The springs at Plombières, a small resort in the Vosges Mountains, were noted for their "waters of fertility," for wives who wanted to become mothers.

Josephine, no less than her husband, after two years of childless marriage, wished for a child. Napoleon's wish was inspired not only by his natural love of children, but also by his Corsican tribal spirit: to sire a large family was a duty to the clan.

As for Josephine, the more the Bonapartes whispered about the possibility of her sterility, the more sensitive she became to the difference in age between her and Napoleon: at twenty-nine, he could expect to father a sizeable family; at thirty-five, her time for child-bearing was running out.

She wanted to please and to hold him. While she had not been as much in love as he at the time of their marriage, she was now beginning to realize how extraordinary a man she had married. She was beginning to see him with the eyes of his men and his officers, who regarded him with awe, who saw him as a

hero, a man of genius, a man of destiny, a man to follow un-
questioningly to the ends of the earth. The sight of him sailing
out of Toulon at the head of that vast expedition may have
stirred her. If she had been reluctant to join him in Italy, she
was eager to join him in Egypt.

But that was not to be.

Weeks were required for news to travel from Egypt to
France; it was weeks before the good news reached her of the
safe landing at Aboukir Bay, the conquest of Alexandria, the
Battle of the Pyramids, the triumphal entry into Cairo.

Bad news travels more quickly, and Josephine next learned
that Nelson's British fleet had surprised the French at anchor,
in a helpless huddle, in Aboukir Bay. Napoleon's hopes soon lay
sunken beside most of France's battleships, fathoms deep below
the waters. With the British in control of the Mediterranean,
there was no way to reinforce or supply his Army of the East.
They were cut off from France, marooned in their own conquest.

It was a good time for France's enemies—England, Austria,
Russia—to combine against her, as they did; they forced France
to retreat to her pre-revolutionary borders and to give up all
that Napoleon had won for her in Italy.

And now a domestic as well as a military crisis confronted
Napoleon. Fresh rumors of his wife's follies and flirtations
finally shattered his confidence. Not only his family, but now

his long-time friend and first aide-de-camp, General Junot, had ugly gossip to report.

Across so many years, it is difficult, today, to know the truth of the charges. But in despair and fury, Napoleon wrote from Cairo to his brother Joseph to tell him that he intended to seek a divorce:

I am undergoing acute domestic distress . . . It is a sad state when one and the same heart is torn by such conflicting sentiments regarding one and the same person. You know what I mean. . . . It is possible that I may be back in France within two months, and I entrust my interests to you. Make arrangements for a country place to be ready for my arrival, either near Paris or in Burgundy . . . I have need of solitude and isolation. Grandeur palls on me . . . Glory stales. At the age of twenty-nine, I have exhausted everything. Life has nothing more to offer . . .

By a quirk of fate, the Bonapartes' private, domestic problem became a public scandal. The French mail ship carrying the General's letter to Joseph was captured by a British patrol-boat and, to the embarrassment of all concerned, published in a London newspaper, later in a Paris one.

If this had not happened, Napoleon might have reconsidered in the months that followed; he had a change of heart, realizing that the accusations against his wife could not be proved and that she had had no chance to defend herself against her attackers.

By mid-summer of 1799, grave national problems arose to demand General Bonaparte's attention. It became clear that the French Republic was imperiled from within as well as from without. There was political conflict at home, civil disorder, economic emergency. The Directors could be neither trusted nor respected. They were dishonest and incompetent. The *Directoire,* as a form of government, had become rotten, and was ready to fall. "The pear was ripe," is how General Bonaparte expressed it, and he decided he would be there to pluck it.

On August eighteenth, he turned over the command in Egypt to General Kléber, and embarked from France with some five hundred men and a handful of his staff, including his stepson and aide-de-camp, Eugene Beauharnais. Somehow his two frigates managed to dodge all the English craft patrolling the Mediterranean, and slipped safely into Fréjus harbor on the French Riviera on October ninth.

The news of their arrival reached Paris the very next night, October tenth, by semaphoric signals, and on October eleventh, Josephine, without so much as a maid, sped out of Paris at daybreak with only Hortense in the carriage beside her. If only she could reach the General first! It would be her first chance—and perhaps her last—to defend herself against her maligners. She would make the most of it.

But as early as her carriage rolled through the gate of the capital, heading south toward Lyon, the Bonaparte brothers were on the road ahead of her.

"In every town and hamlet as we drove along," in Hortense's words, "we saw arches of triumph being raised, and whenever we stopped for a change of horses, people crowded about our carriage to ask if it was true that the Savior was on his way—for that was the name by which all France hailed the General at that hour. Beset by foreign defeats and domestic turmoil, with the treasury depleted and the *Directoire* in disrepute, the nation saw General Bonaparte's return as a blessing from heaven. His passage all the way to Paris was one long triumph —a sign to him and to his enemies of what France expected of him."

Hoping to catch a glimpse of him, men lined the roads, standing throughout the night with torches to light his way back to the capital. A tingle of joy, relief, and hope raced along the network of highroads and byroads. The wave of excitement and adulation must have affected Josephine as it did Hortense. Though she was late in realizing that she was married to an extraordinary man, she realized it fully now, going to this meeting with him more eagerly, more yearningly than to any in all their years of courtship and marriage.

Part III

Sad to say, she missed him—he taking one road north, while she traveled south on another. "With the unfortunate result that we arrived in Paris two days ahead of her," relates Eugene, who was accompanying the General. "Time enough for her enemies! They turned it to their advantage, seizing on the opportunity of her absence from home to further injure her in her husband's estimation, to poison his mind, to turn him against her."

"They" were Napoleon's mother, his brothers, and his sisters. They even tried to make him believe that Josephine had run away with a lover.

When she finally realized that she had missed him on the road, turned her horses around, and retraced the two hundred miles back to Paris, she found her husband's door locked and bolted against her. All her pleas, all her sobs, all the night long, could not persuade him to open it.

With the dawn, Josephine abandoned hope and admitted defeat, difficult as it was for her to accept the fact that, for the first time in their three and a half years of marriage, her husband could withstand her tears, her entreaties, her promises, her allurements. She had started down the stairs in final retreat when her maid came up, leading Hortense and Eugene by the hand, urging her mistress to make one last appeal, with the children to plead her cause.

It was the voices of the children that softened the General's

heart, shook him in his iron resolve. With a stern face, with reddened eyes which betrayed his own weeping, he opened his arms to Eugene, to Hortense . . . and, finally, to Josephine. The reconciliation had been accomplished. At the crucial hour, Josephine's magic had not failed her.

Josephine was at her husband's side as he planned the coup d'état whereby he would seize control of the government. With the aid of his brothers and a group of his devoted fellow-officers, he succeeded in overthrowing the *Directoire* in November of 1799. Power was transferred to a Consulate, an executive committee of three men, three Consuls, in the ancient Roman tradition, with General Bonaparte as one of the three, the foremost, the First Consul.

The new constitution and the Consulate were put to the vote of the people, and approved by a national referendum in early 1800.

After eleven years of revolution and disorder, the entire structure of national law, administration, finance, and education awaited rebuilding by Napoleon. The old order had been torn down, a new order had to be erected in its place. As First Consul and later as Emperor, Napoleon proceeded to this task with formidable speed, efficiency, and wisdom. His genius was not only military but political as well; he now furnished proof of his brilliant legislative, organizational, and administrative powers.

In February of 1800 the First Consul and his First Lady moved into the Tuileries Palace, from which the King and Queen of France had been driven by angry mobs only eight years earlier. Bloodstains left by that fierce struggle were scrubbed from the parquet floors, and the royal suite redecorated, at Josephine's orders, in the latest fashion, an Egyptian theme—sphinx heads and claws, lotus flowers, hieroglyphics—in compliment to the conqueror of the Nile.

On the night of February seventeenth, after the first splendid official consular reception in the palace, the First Consul pulled up a stool before the huge, high, bronze-trimmed mahogany bed and said with a smile to his lady: "Come, little Creole, step up into the bed of your former masters." True or not, that is how the story is told by Josephine's friend and confidante, Claire de Rémusat, who says she heard it from Josephine herself.

A shiver must have run up and down Josephine's spine at her husband's teasing. She was a very superstitious woman. Here she was sleeping in the bed of Queen Marie Antoinette! Would she sit on the Queen's throne, as well? Was it possible that Euphémie could have seen all of this in the lines of her palm, twenty or more years ahead of time?

"My mother was obsessed with the thought of Marie Antoinette," Hortense wrote in her *Memoirs,* "and saw her tragic figure everywhere. The Palace seemed haunted by the Poor Queen. My mother upset me when she said, 'I know I shall not be happy here. The darkest forebodings came over me the moment I entered.' "

But she was still happy at that hour. In the fourth year of their marriage, Napoleon and Josephine seemed to have come upon smooth sailing, the stormy seas safely past. The necessary concessions and adjustments had been made, one to the other. If Napoleon was no longer head over heels in love, his love was steadier. He was filled with deep devotion and tenderness for his wife.

She was his perfect mate temperamentally as well as physically, melting as smoothly and gracefully into his moods as into his arms. She had become profoundly necessary to him. He turned to her for comfort, sympathy, diversion, and, above all, for relaxation from the terrible tensions that racked him. It was Josephine he called for when he left his study at night, to read him to sleep in her deliciously soothing, honey-sweet voice. And, at his summons, she deserted all the guests in her apartment, left her game of billiards, whist, or backgammon to rush to his bedside. It was Josephine who diverted him at lunchtime or at dinner with her frivolous chatter, her soufflé of scandal whipped up just for his entertainment.

He would leave the council table or his desk, physically and mentally weary, and come clattering down his back staircase to seek out Josephine. He loved to visit her at her dressing table, charging in like a bull in a china shop, upsetting crystal perfume bottles, overturning trays of laces and feathers, and "turning her jewel cases topsy-turvy," according to her favorite maid, still another person who wrote the memoirs of her life with the Empress. "He hovered over her, giving her love-pats sharp enough to bring tears to her eyes, although her only reproach, in that soft sweet drawl of hers, was a mild, 'That's enough, now, Bonaparte, that's enough!'"

Josephine also played a second important role in Napoleon's life and destiny—that of ideal wife or consort to the head of state, for her social talents complemented his political genius. Her graciousness and gentleness attracted to his court a great number of people who would otherwise have been frightened off or offended by his natural brusqueness. When the First Consul stormed in and out, his face alternating between the irresistible smile that lightened it and the fierce scowl that darkened it, Josephine stood by, the soul of tact, to mend wounded pride and injured feelings. Hers was the soft answer, the gentle touch, the healing smile and the infectious ripple of laughter that relieved tension.

Josephine was useful, too, on the international level, where it was necessary that France regain her social prestige as she had regained her military and political standing. With the suc-

cess of the first glittering reception at which Josephine welcomed the diplomatic corps to her apartments in the Tuileries,
Napoleon was assured of realizing his ambition to make the
French court once again the paragon of elegance for all Europe,
all the world. Josephine managed to mold an impressive consular court out of Napoleon's crude, predominantly military en-
tourage.

She set herself to the study of protocol—the science of court
ceremonial—and mastered it. She memorized the name, rank,
and title of every member of every noble and royal house in
Europe; she knew which prince or duke was to be greeted first
at palace receptions, who should walk ahead of whom in royal
processions. Never once did she make a mistake in that highly
complicated business of court etiquette.

In May of that same year of 1800, Napoleon successfully led
a whirlwind, thirty-day campaign into Italy to take back from
the Austrians the territories they had taken back from France.

France made a triumph of his homecoming, voices rang out
in endless cries of *Vive le Général,* Long Live the General!
"Acclamations as sweet in my ears as the sound of Josephine's
voice!" he told his secretary.

A grateful, jubilant nation, by 1802, voted to make General
Bonaparte the First Consul for life, with the privilege of desig-
nating his successor.

Paris celebrated the occasion with city-wide illumination,

with concerts and fireworks, including Napoleon's five-pointed star, thirty feet in height, gleaming throughout the night above the towers of Notre Dame Cathedral.

It was a tremendous honor, to be sure, and one in which Josephine delighted, except for the fact that it brought up the touchy subject of a successor, a son and heir to follow his father as France's head of state.

The Bonapartes returned to the attack on Josephine, the wife who was still not a mother after several years of marriage. They hoped that Napoleon would keep his supreme power in the family.

Brother Lucien, on a diplomatic mission in Madrid, submitted a proposal from the Queen of Spain to the First Consul, suggesting that he take a Spanish princess as his bride. The Infanta Isabel, at thirteen years of age, had all her child-bearing years ahead of her the Queen said, and could supply royal blood to the new Bonaparte line of rulers—if the First Consul decided to found one.

Napoleon reproached Lucien for meddling in his personal affairs, adding that if he decided to take a royal bride for political reasons, it would not be from a weak and powerless nation such as Spain.

Josephine, mild, soft-spoken, slow to anger, shrank from the increasingly sharp and bitter family arguments.

100

Part III

She went back to Plombières for the waters, back and back again, but that hope soon failed her. The doctors' pills and tonics were no better. Her prayers produced no miracle. Deep in her thirties, a miracle was what she needed.

In 1801, she thought she had hit upon a solution to the problem of a successor: the marriage of her daughter Hortense to her husband's brother Louis, which, she argued, would protect her own marriage to Napoleon. Louis was the brother closest to Napoleon's heart, the one most likely to be chosen as his successor. The marriage also held out a promise of compatability in ages and tastes: Louis, twenty-three, Hortense, eighteen; both artistically inclined—Hortense an artist and composer, Louis a would-be novelist and poet. Louis had already shown some interest in Hortense who, though not as pretty as her mother, had a halo of fair hair, violent-blue eyes, and a lovely, graceful figure.

It took a great deal of persuasion to talk Hortense into the match. Her head was still full of ideal romantic notions, she was reluctant at the thought of the reality of matrimony. But Josephine felt justified in forcing the issue: she herself had been a wife and mother at her daughter's age, and if Josephine's parents had arranged her marriage, Hortense could expect the same. Times had not yet changed, in that respect.

Josephine knew that Louis was frail and delicate, but she did not know that he would become an invalid, in body and

101

mind, a sad neurotic, subject to spells of melancholy and fits of jealousy. Before it was all over, he would bring his wife, Hortense, to utter despair, to the verge of breakdown.

While the family hoped that the marriage would go better after the birth of Louis's and Hortense's first child late in 1802, their hopes were doomed to disappointment. Napoleon and Josephine were consoled, however, by the fact that the child was a boy, christened Napoleon Charles, and a great favorite of his uncle.

And Josephine had not yet abandoned all hope for a child of her own. She went off in a different direction, to another mineral springs, this time to Aix-la-Chapelle, under the supervision of the court physician. Her husband was as eager and hopeful as she. A child of his very own would be the *ideal* solution to the problem of succession.

At the hour when the Senate of France was to proclaim Napoleon Bonaparte Emperor of the Republic—a title preferred by him to that of king because, as he said, he found it "even grander, more stirring to the imagination"—the question of an heir loomed larger than at any time before. Several months later, by popular vote, the French people approved the Senate action, confirmed Napoleon as Emperor Napoleon I, to be succeeded, of course, by his own legitimate son, if he could produce one; if not, by a son of his brother Prince Louis or brother Prince Joseph—all the Bonapartes now princes and princesses.

Another provision of the confirmation cheered Josephine: Napoleon was privileged to adopt one of his nephews and to designate him as son and heir. It was Napoleon Charles, the son of Louis and Hortense, upon whom Josephine had set her heart as adoptive son and heir, and certainly Napoleon seemed to favor that child. But Louis refused, turning upon them in a rage and screaming that he would never permit his son to be advanced to a position outranking his own and demanding to know why he should have been passed over as direct successor to his brother.

The date for the coronation was set: December 2, 1804. The Pope himself would come from Rome to Paris to perform the sacred ceremony.

The question was: would Josephine have a place in the proceedings? Or would Napoleon divorce her before that date came around? There was every indication that he would. Certainly, if it was his intention to do so, he should do it before, not after, she had been crowned Empress of France.

Prince Joseph argued that Josephine should attend the coronation merely as a spectator, since her consecration as Empress by the hand of the Holy Father would further complicate the divorce which he and the Bonapartes considered unavoidable.

Napoleon managed, before the ceremony, to tell Josephine

that it was his responsibility as Emperor of France to marry a woman capable of giving him and the nation a successor. A break in the line of rulers would give rise to new disorder, more civil war—between Bonapartists, Royalists, and Republicans. He pointed out how vitally necessary a divorce had become in the light of his new imperial position.

"I lack the courage to make the decision," he told her, "and if you display too great an affliction, if you refuse to act except in obedience to my command, I know I shall never be able to bring myself to speak it. I must tell you, however, that I do ardently wish that you, yourself, would withdraw in the national interest, and to spare me the pain of forcing the issue." Napoleon wept as he spoke.

Josephine's answer to her husband was that she stood ready to obey if he demanded a divorce, but that she herself would never take the initiative. Sad, tender, gentle, sweet, submissive, taking the attitude of an unresisting victim, she brought her husband to a state of agitation and uncertainty from which he could not recover.

Finally, pushed too far by his scheming family, and resentful of them, he suddenly announced to his wife that the Pope was on his way from Rome to Paris and would crown them both. She was to proceed immediately to make her preparations for the coronation.

PART
IV

What better way is there to hear about the coronation of Napoleon than in the words of someone who actually saw it? Madame Junot, who later recorded her impressions of the ceremony, was present in Notre Dame Cathedral on that occasion, standing close to the altar with her husband, one of Napoleon's favorite generals. Or to hear it described by someone who actually took part in the ceremony? Such a person is Claire de Rémusat, who became one of Josephine's court ladies.

The Empress, Claire de Rémusat tells us in her memoirs, *called in the greatest artists of the day to confer with her on the design of the official costume for the court ladies, as well as of her own: the long mantle to cover our dresses, the gold or silver embroidered lace ruff, rising high from the shoulders to frame the neck and face. At this point, we Ladies of the Court suddenly discovered that our education had been neglected. We did not know how to make a proper bow. So, the*

*dancing master to the former queen was called in to teach us
how to approach the throne and curtsy to the monarch. Next
came rehearsals of the highly complicated coronation ritual,
with the court painter David to direct the principal figures in
their movements, designing the living tableau of the rite as he
would later put it on canvas. It still seems a dream, one of
Oriental splendor straight out of* The Arabian Nights.

*It is impossible to imagine the excitement, the gaiety and
the revelry in Paris at the time!* Madame Junot exclaims. *The
streets were thronged from morning to night with a joyous,
hustling, bustling multitude . . . some rushing to try to secure
tickets for the ceremony, others to engage windows along the
route of the procession, from which to watch it pass. Before
daybreak on the second of December, all Paris was awake and
stirring, hundreds never having gone to bed.*

At nine o'clock, as Claire de Rémusat takes over the story,
*the great golden coach, drawn by eight bay horses and sur-
mounted by a crown and four spread-winged imperial eagles,
passed through the gates of the Tuileries Palace, the Emperor
and Empress seated on its white velvet cushions. She, re-
splendent in diamonds, wore a diamond bandeau in her hair,
which was arranged in a mass of ringlets, and a gown and
court cape of white satin embroidered in gold and silver . . .
wearing all this with her customary style, and looking not a
day over twenty-five. The Emperor was dazzling, too, in crim-*

110

son velvet, which would later be exchanged for the imperial garments upon arrival at the Cathedral. There, the great ermine cloak would be placed upon his shoulders, the Caesar's golden laurel crown upon his head.

Who that saw Notre Dame Cathedral on that memorable day could ever forget it? Madame Junot asks in her memoirs. *The walls were hung with glowing tapestries and adorned with flowers; the vaulted ceiling re-echoed the chant of the priests and the voices of the choir. All the representatives of France were there assembled: the military men in their bright colored uniforms, senators and tribunes in plumed hats, the clergy in their handsome flowing robes, the young and beautiful women sparkling with jewels and dressed in a style and elegance to be seen only in Paris. On his arrival at Notre Dame, Napoleon ascended the steps to the throne in front of the high altar. The Pope anointed his hands and brow with the sacred oil and gave the benediction. But at the moment when His Holiness reached for the crown of Charlemagne to take it from the altar, Napoleon seized it in his own hands and placed it upon his own head. He was strikingly handsome at that moment.*

Then it was Josephine's turn to descend from her throne and advance toward the altar, Madame de Rémusat continues, *followed by her retinue of court ladies, her scarlet velvet train borne by the three Bonaparte Princesses, Caroline, Pauline*

111

and Elisa. *One of Josephine's chief beauties, in addition to her exquisite figure, was the graceful tilt of her neck, the elegant carriage of her head; indeed, her entire bearing was notable for grace and dignity. And I could read in Napoleon's face the confirmation of my observation. He looked with an air of proud satisfaction at his Empress as she advanced toward him and the altar. And when she knelt down, when the tears she could not hold back fell upon her clasped hands raised to heaven—or, rather, to Napoleon—both he and she appeared to enjoy one of those brief moments of pure bliss that come once in a lifetime.*

The Emperor performed every action of that complicated ceremony with remarkable grace. Madame Junot, standing within a few feet of the sovereigns, observes: *But his manner of crowning Josephine was the most striking. After receiving the small crown surmounted by the cross, he had to place it on his head first and then to transfer it to that of the Empress. When the moment arrived for her coronation, his manner was almost sportive. He took great pains to arrange this little crown over Josephine's tiara of diamonds, putting it on, taking it off, and finally putting it on again, as if to promise her that she should wear it gracefully and lightly.*

After the Empress had risen from her knees to move back to the throne, Claire de Rémusat again takes up the story, *the three Bonaparte Princesses purposely dropped the Empress's*

112

ermine-lined velvet train, so that the full weight of it fell against her, with the result that she almost staggered and fell as she mounted the steps to the throne. His sisters' action had not escaped their brother's eagle eye, and he hissed a low but effective warning, so that they picked up the Empress's train again.

As the ceremony ended, as the mighty voice of the organ swelled and joined the voices of the choir to fill the vastness of the cathedral with joyous sound, did Josephine hear—in the music—the words "More than queen," spoken so many long years before?

The imperial procession did not arrive back at the Tuileries Palace until after dark on that December evening . . . its way illumined by torches, Claire de Rémusat remembers. *The Emperor, in a gay and charming mood, insisted that the Empress keep on her little crown, even though they dined alone, just the two of them, in their private apartments. He lavished compliments on her for the distinction with which she wore it.*

As Emperor and Empress they were elevated to a position so lofty as to be lonely; they were alone together in a solitary splendor, with the result that they drew closer to each other. Sharing the throne with Napoleon, Josephine proved his indispensable companion and confidante. As he became more and more dependent upon her, he evinced an ever greater tenderness toward her. After the coronation, he was addressed as Your Majesty or Sire by all the court. Only Josephine still dared to call him Bonaparte . . . only she and the trained parrot that she had taught to shriek that name. Since the impudent red and green bird could not be broken of the habit, he had to be exiled to the servants' quarters, a gift to Josephine's favorite maid, who tells the story.

To Napoleon's pride and pleasure, Josephine made a success of her role as sovereign and royal consort. "I have had the honor," Madame Junot wrote, "of being presented to many real princesses of royal blood, but I never saw one who presented so perfect a personification of elegance and majesty as did the Empress Josephine."

Josephine worked hard at her job. If her first husband had accused her of laziness and indifference to learning, she now proved him wrong. With the aid of an expert tutor, she began a course in the history and tradition of all the nations and courts of Europe, including the family trees of all the royal houses. No queen of France before her was ever more knowledgeable in these subjects.

In 1805, honors were lavished on Josephine and her children, the Bonapartes seething with resentment to see the hated Beauharnais family attain such heights. Napoleon named Eugene Vice-Arch-Chancellor of the Empire and praised him warmly as "one of the pillars of our throne, one of the staunchest defenders of our realm." Hortense's second son, Napoleon Louis, had the honor of being christened by the Pope himself, while her first son, Napoleon Charles, now a handsome fellow of three, appeared to be the Emperor's favorite, a favoritism unlikely to please the parents of his other nieces and nephews. It was this namesake whom the Emperor bounced on his knee at the table, who was fed tidbits from the imperial plate, given sips of wine or coffee from the imperial cup, and indulged even to the point of being allowed to wear the sword of state—strutting and stumbling about the room with the great scabbard strapped about his neck. It was a performance which amused Napoleon enormously and which, happily, the artist Baron Gérard captured in a portrait commissioned by Josephine.

The crown of France was not enough for Napoleon, and in 1805, in the Cathedral at Milan, he also put on that of Italy. Josephine became not only Empress of France, but also Queen of Italy.

When her son, Eugene, was appointed Viceroy of that country, Josephine swelled with pride until she realized that it meant parting from this beloved son, who would have to stay on in Italy to head the government.

The next year, Napoleon formally adopted Eugene as his son, named him a Prince of France, and promised him the crown of Italy as his inheritance.

As a prince, Eugene could marry a princess, and soon did: Princess Amalie Augusta, daughter of the King of Bavaria. "No one could be prettier than this princess!" Josephine wrote enthusiastically to her son who had not yet seen the bride selected for him by Napoleon. No one could have been nicer, either, or sweeter or brighter, so this prince and princess lived happily ever after, in the best fairy-tale tradition—most unusual for a royal marriage arranged solely for reasons of state, for the purpose of international relations.

Next, Josephine was to see her daughter Hortense crowned queen, Queen of Holland, sharing that throne with her husband, Louis, whom Napoleon named king. And as the Emperor's conquests continued, he had thrones enough to go around for almost all the family: that of Spain for brother Joseph, that of Naples for sister Caroline, that of Westphalia for Jerome, the baby of the family.

Hortense's and Louis's marriage went no better in the palace at Amsterdam than it had in the house in Paris. Hortense was even unhappier as Louis's queen than as his wife. "She was," as one friend remarked, "the unhappiest woman of her time." A throne was the very last thing she had wanted: it was, she wrote, "the cruelest ordeal of all those fate had in store for me."

One of the cruel blows of fate was the sudden death by croup of her four-year-old son, Napoleon Charles. She went into a state of shock, she could not weep a tear, nor speak a word, even to Josephine, who rushed to Belgium to meet her stricken daughter and escort her back to France to recuperate.

Josephine was learning that glory for herself and her family did not mean happiness or peace of mind. As she told a friend, it was no fun to wear a crown. "The crown had literally as well as figuratively hurt her head," as the friend repeated the conversation. "The Empress told me that even though she wore an inner velvet band under it, the heavy crown always left painful, red marks on her forehead."

Josephine commiserated with her daughter in her illness and her loss. Little Napoleon Charles would not succeed his uncle as emperor but, fortunately, there was still little Napoleon Louis to take his brother's place as heir to the French empire.

She also sorrowed over her separation from Eugene and his family, in far off Milan.

And she grieved over the constant wars in which France and Napoleon were involved. Once, she must have written him a letter—though it has been lost—asking whether he could do nothing but fight? We have his reply which is rather huffy:

"Yes, I know how to do something else besides making war, as you put it! I, too, yearn to return to Paris, to you, to a peaceful life, but duty comes first, and all my life I have sacrificed my personal pleasure and happiness to my Destiny."

France's enemies banded together again and again to fight off France's ever increasing power and domination over Europe. England, Austria, and Russia headed the several coalitions and tried to induce the other, smaller European nations to join with them to resist the pressures of the ambitious Napoleon and his thus far irresistible French legions.

Josephine pleaded to be allowed to accompany her husband on his campaigns up and down the continent of Europe. Not to the front lines, of course, but part of the way, at least—although to keep up with the Emperor in his travels was almost too much for any woman. On one trip from Italy to Paris, he insisted on such breakneck speed that at every relay station, while the exhausted and lathered horses were removed from their traces to make way for fresh ones, buckets of water had to be poured over the smoking-hot carriage wheels. And this was one of the Emperor's non-stop journeys, as he had warned the Empress when she had begged to ride with him. Her maid complained bitterly of the hardships, describing how her "legs and feet became painfully puffed and swollen from the long days and nights jolting in a carriage." It is doubtful Josephine fared much better than the maid, riding in the carriage behind the imperial coach, with the Emperor's valet. But even with all 'her husband's galloping back and forth across the continent, over thousands of miles, Josephine never willingly stayed behind, never willingly parted from him.

The victories had piled up through so many years that France came to take them for granted. Not Josephine. She suffered agonies of anxiety while she waited for messages from the battle zone. In 1806, in her palace at Mainz, near Frankfurt, where the Emperor had left her while he and the army drove toward Berlin, she sat up night after night, laying out the cards for the various kinds of solitaire which she used for fortune-telling. Hers were ordinary decks of playing cards, not the mysterious and ancient Tarot cards which are usually used to predict the future. She was still as superstitious as she had been as a girl, in the Islands. Success in her three favorite games—the Great Patience, the Little Patience, and the Windmill—was interpreted by Josephine as a symbol of success for her husband and the French forces.

Late one night in October, she won all three in a row and called out in high excitement to her Ladies of the Palace: "This means we are soon to hear good news from the battlefront, some incredibly great victory!" No sooner had she spoken these words than a horse could be heard clattering into the courtyard, and a footman announced a messenger from the

Emperor. The messenger entered in his mud-spattered uniform and knelt to present the letter to the Empress: "My dear Josephine, we have met the Prussian army and it no longer exists. I am well, and press you to my heart."

Sometimes, the Emperor sent for Josephine to join him in the wake of his conquests, as in Munich in 1805. As she traveled across southern Germany on her way to Bavaria, cannons boomed, church bells rang, and bands blared in greeting to her. Her greeting, in return, was always warm, gracious. Those who came to gape at Josephine fell subject to her charm and radiance. The story of her passage through the Black Forest is one which the peasants told to their children—and their children, in turn, to their own—so that a hundred years later a legend had grown up in the region about the French Empress who had appeared among them "like a fairy queen, glittering in diamonds and pearls, in a cloak the color of dawn and a gown the color of sunlight."

"I win battles, Josephine wins hearts," Napoleon said to his secretary when told of the enthusiasm and admiration evoked by his wife along her path.

There were still occasional, brief happy moments such as these for Josephine, but the specter of divorce continued to haunt her, year in, year out. As she could clearly see, there were many beautiful young women in the

Emperor's life; but it was not these passing fancies, these rivals in her court she feared as much as she did the unseen, unknown, shadowy figures—the princesses of foreign lands being proposed to Napoleon by his family and his ambassadors as suitable brides of an emperor.

Josephine knew that her husband was looking over the field of eligible royal candidates, that he had gone to Rome to inspect Eugene's sister-in-law, Princess Charlotte of Bavaria, who failed, however, to capture his fancy. Josephine heard too that the Emperor had stopped in Dresden to meet the daughter of the King of Saxony, but she proved neither young enough (at thirty) nor pretty enough to appeal to him romantically. And certainly, from the viewpoint of international politics, her father's small kingdom could offer no advantage; so she, too, was crossed off the list of matrimonial prospects.

Finally, the field of princesses narrowed down to two: a grand duchess of Russia and an archduchess of Austria, the only two alliances representative of genuine diplomatic significance.

In November of 1809, Napoleon sent an ambassador to the Court of St. Petersburg to make formal request to the Czar of Russia for the hand in marriage of his fourteen-year-old sister, the Grand Duchess Anna.

At the same time, Napoleon sent a message to Eugene in Italy asking him to come immediately to France. He wanted

Eugene to help him break the news to Josephine. The conqueror of Europe could not gather up the courage to tell his wife that he had decided on divorce, that he wanted to remarry, to have a child of his own—not of his brothers'—to whom to leave this great empire he had built.

Napoleon despised himself for his weakness in dealing with Josephine. This was almost the only time in his entire career that he failed to deal swiftly, efficiently, and ruthlessly with the obstacle that blocked his path.

He finally brought himself to speak the words, to make the announcement to his wife at dinner on November 30, 1809, as they sat alone in his apartment in the Tuileries Palace.

"No, no!" she cried, "I will never survive it!" and fainted dead away, her limp form to be lifted off the floor and carried up a secret staircase to her apartment by the Emperor and Count de Bausset, the Prefect of the Palace, who promptly wrote down every word, published later in his book *Anecdotes from Inside the Palace*.

Napoleon summoned the doctor and Hortense to the Empress's bedside.

"It is for the best," Hortense said to soothe her mother. *"We will all go away . . . and, for the first time in our lives, far from the world and the court, in some peaceful retreat, we will live a real family life and know our first real happiness."*

But Napoleon would not hear of the idea of Hortense's and Eugene's departure from the court.

"I need you," he declared to them. "Nor is it your mother's wish that you should separate yourselves and your children from me. Were you to leave me, it might well appear that your mother had been repudiated for some just cause. Whereas, as I foresee it, her position is to be one of dignity and honor. Here is proof to history that the divorce is purely a political one, one to which she herself agrees and by which she will win even greater respect, esteem and gratitude from the nation for which she sacrifices herself."

The divorce settlement was as generous as Napoleon had promised: Josephine would retain her rank and title of Queen and Empress with all the honors, privileges, and distinctions she had previously enjoyed. She would still be addressed as Your Majesty, her carriage would still be drawn by eight horses, as was the Emperor's, with the same imperial crest on the door, and with fourteen uniformed horsemen and a trumpeter riding alongside. She would continue to be surrounded by a large honor household, her one hundred and seventy servants—one footman behind every chair at her table—would continue to wear the imperial colors. She was, of course, to keep her personal property and her beautiful estate of Malmaison, near Paris. As her Paris residence, she was to have the Elysée

Palace, where the President of France makes his headquarters today. She was to have a yearly allowance of three million francs, and all her current debts—which were enormous— were to be paid separately by the Emperor. He offered to make her a ruler in her own right, with a capital city such as Rome or Brussels, with a palace and court of her own, but she went into hysterics at the very mention of leaving Paris, re- minding him of his promise that she was to be permitted to stay in France, preferably in Paris, close to him. She had no desire for kingdoms or power for herself, only for her children and grandchildren.

The imperial divorce was treated as an affair of state. The official ceremony was to take place on December fifteenth, and the guests were invited, as to a ball, by formal invitation, over the signature of the Grand Chamberlain of the Empire: "I have the honor to advise Your Excellency that the Emperor re- quires your presence at nine o'clock in the Throne Room of the Palace of the Tuileries." On that day, the princes and princesses of the imperial family and the state officials, all in full court dress, were ushered into the Throne Room and seated accord- ing to rank.

The Emperor spoke first and announced his decision:

I have found courage for it only in the conviction that it serves the best interests of France. . . . I have only gratitude

*to express for the devotion and tenderness of my well-beloved
wife. She has embellished thirteen years of my life, and the
memory will remain forever engraved upon my heart.*

The Paris newspaper, printing his words the next day,
made mention that "the Emperor wept."

Next came Josephine's turn; she began to read the speech
written out for her:

*I wish to declare that, having lost all hope of bearing chil-
dren who could satisfy my husband's need of an heir to his
throne, I proudly offer to him the greatest proof of attachment
and devotion ever given a husband on this earth.*

At this point, Josephine's strength and voice failed her, and
she collapsed, sobbing, into her chair. The Secretary of State
had to finish reading the text for her, down to the last line:
"My husband and I stand glorified by this sacrifice we make for
the sake of the national welfare."

But she was not to get off so easily; the ordeal dragged on.
The official record of the proceedings had to be signed by the
Emperor and the Empress and all ten members of the Bona-
parte-Beauharnais families. Only then was Josephine free to
leave the scene of her humiliation.

"The Emperor," Hortense tells us, "kissed her, took her by
the hand and led her to her apartments."

PART V

The day after the ceremony, at two o'clock, the Empress was to leave the Palace of the Tuileries forever.

Tears were in every eye, her maid writes of the departure, as she went out carrying what she called her "menagerie," the green and red parrot in a cage and a basketful of new-born puppies. *The Empress had been so kind to everyone. Who among the Emperor's staff did not consider her their friend and protector? It was to her that everyone turned to ask a special favor or a pardon. . . . Her children did not leave her side during those cruel hours. Prince Eugene made a noble effort to pretend a gaiety he could not feel, and told funny stories to make us smile.*

Hortense tried to tell her mother that things could have been worse, reminding her that when poor Queen Marie Antoinette had made her departure from this palace it was in the direction of prison and the guillotine . . . whereas Empress Josephine was on her way to her beloved country house, her Château de Malmaison.

Even so, her tears continued to flow. For which Napoleon reproached her when he came to visit, two days later, to walk with her in the gardens, in full view of his military staff and her ladies, standing by at a respectful distance.

I was heartsick at sight of you, Napoleon wrote soon after; in those first weeks he wrote almost daily. *I hear that you are still weeping . . . That is awful . . . I will come back to see you when you can assure me you are in a more cheerful frame of mind . . . You must not allow yourself to become melancholy . . . You should realize that I cannot be happy unless I know you are.*

Happy she would never be again. "Sometimes I have the feeling that I am dead," she told her friend Claire de Rémusat, "and that the only sign of life remaining is the hazy sensation that I no longer exist."

"She is so gentle and affectionate in her sorrow," Claire wrote her husband, "that it breaks my heart to see her. Never a word of bitterness or complaint escapes her lips. She is truly as sweet as an angel."

Within a month after the divorce, the next Empress was chosen: the Archduchess Marie Louise, daughter of the Habsburg Emperor of Austria, blue-eyed, fair, plump, not unattractive, just nineteen years old.

The Austrian match had been made when it became clear to Napoleon that the Russian one would never be consummated. The Czar had been elusive from the beginning—never giving an outright No, but never a definite Yes. His mother, the Dowager Empress, adamantly opposed a marital alliance between the imperial Romanovs and the upstart Bonapartes. The Habsburg Emperor, however, felt he could not afford to offend this powerful neighbor, just across the Rhine, by refusing him his daughter's hand in marriage.

By February, the marriage contracts had been signed, Napoleon had asked Hortense to give him lessons in the waltz, lavish gifts and jewels had been sent off by the groom to the bride in Vienna, and elaborate festivities planned for her reception in Paris. On April second she made her triumphal entry into the French capital. The marriage was celebrated in the presence of eight thousand guests in the chapel of the Tuileries.

Not the faintest echo of the cannon booming welcome to the new Empress in Paris could be heard by the old Empress in exile in Normandy. It was not actually exile, though it amounted to much the same thing: Napoleon had recently given Josephine a princely domain near Evreux with a huge and old and dank and crumbling castle—the last thing she ever wanted, sixty miles—thirteen posting stations—removed from

Paris. However, this distance was the very reason for Napoleon's generosity, the Austrian Ambassador having suggested that it would be indelicate for the Emperor to have his first wife so close by as he greeted the arrival of his second.

It was only to be expected that the lords and ladies of the court would compare the first wife and the second, the old empress and the new . . . all in favor of the old. Josephine had been gentle, cordial, kind, where Marie Louise was "cold and haughty," in Claire de Rémusat's opinion. The new Empress looked down her long Habsburg nose at those without royal blood in their veins, including, probably, even the Bonapartes. She was an Austrian and found difficulty pronouncing the names of the French nobility—those few, that is, that she bothered to remember. As a result, she was no more popular in France than was her great-aunt, Marie Antoinette, whose fate apparently did not daunt her.

If Marie Louise felt any misgivings about coming to France, they probably concerned the man whom she was to wed, for he was "the ogre" of her childhood: twice in the preceding five years he had chased her and her family out of their palace, out of their capital city of Vienna, when he marched in with his conquering armies.

But now the "ogre" set himself to please her, proved a fond and indulgent husband. And when she announced to him, as

134

she shortly did, that she was expecting their child, his affection knew no bounds.

When their child was born on March 20, 1811, a salvo of a hundred guns announced a boy, the son and heir for whom the Emperor and the Empire had longed—the King of Rome!

Napoleon immediately sent off a message to Normandy, to Josephine, to tell her of the great event: "My son is big and sturdy. I hope he will develop well. He has my chest, my mouth and eyes. I hope he will fulfill his destiny." If the horseman who galloped out of Paris that morning and rode hard for six hours to deliver the Emperor's hand-written letter expected a handsome reward from the Empress, he was not disappointed: she presented him with a magnificent diamond decoration, its intrinsic value further enhanced by the gracious manner of the giver.

"The Empress showed the most lively and apparently the most sincere delight as she read the Emperor's letter," according to her maid. "In this blessing to the nation, I reap the reward of my sacrifice," Josephine is quoted as saying.

She was to see the child only once, and then without his mother's knowledge. Napoleon had to arrange with the royal governess to take the little King of Rome to a remote corner of a Paris park for a secret meeting with Josephine. "The Empress went down on her knees before the child," the governess wrote later, "burst into tears and kissed his hands, saying, 'Sweet child, one day you will know what a sacrifice I made for you.' "

After the divorce, it gave Josephine great pleasure to have children come to visit her at Malmaison, to brighten her lonely hours. Above all, she enjoyed seeing her own grandchildren, especially Hortense's two boys. After their first son died, Hortense and Louis had had another son, in 1808, Charles Louis Napoleon, another namesake of the Emperor's, the one who would finally come to the throne of France in 1851 as Napoleon III. (When he did, he made Malmaison into a museum, a national shrine in memory of his beloved grandmother.)

Hortense was happy again during these years, for she was free, at last, from both her husband and the throne of Holland. Louis and Napoleon had disagreed on Dutch national policy; clearly, the King of Holland could not long stand up against the Emperor of France, so Louis had abdicated, departed Amsterdam in a tantrum, and gone to live in Germany. Hortense then went her own way, with the children. Her way led back to France, close to her mother.

"*Maman,* you indulge us when we are good," Hortense's youngest son told her, "but *Grand'maman* spoils us *all* the time!" And probably she did, with constant gifts, the most costly and unusual toys she could find in Paris or order from

136

Germany—such as a pair of tiny golden hens that laid tiny silver eggs. She indulged them with chocolates, bonbons, and marzipan, with carriage drives and fishing expeditions, with daily visits to the Malmaison zoo where there were kangaroos, flying squirrels, ostriches, storks and imperial eagles, and, best of all, a trained orangutan that slept in a bed, wearing a nightdress, and ate at a table, dressed in a fashionable long coat, politely handling a knife and fork.

The menagerie was amusing for young visitors, but grown-up visitors came from all over the world to see the hothouses for which Malmaison was famous. Josephine had been homesick for her island home and island flowers—the brilliantly colored, tropic flora of her native Martinique—and so she had sent for pots of familiar shrubs and plants from the Trois Ilets gardens. For a woman to take up gardening was more unusual in her day than in ours. But she worked at it as a science; she studied with botanists and supervised her gardeners. French army and naval officers, ambassadors and foreign potentates vied with one another to find rare specimens with which to surprise the Empress. Thanks to her efforts, between 1804 and 1814 some one hundred and eighty species of flowers blossomed on French soil for the first time. Among them were camellia, mimosa, purple magnolia, rhododendron, geranium, phlox, dahlia, and hibiscus. Public parks and private gardens all over Europe bloomed anew through the seed packets, the cuttings,

and the bulbs that could be had for the asking from Malmaison. For the fact that France became a flower bower and the French, a nation of flower lovers, much credit is due to Josephine.

Along with the greenhouses and gardens, Malmaison's art gallery also enjoyed world fame, with its two hundred superb paintings by French, Dutch, and Italian masters. A connoisseur of art, Josephine had begun her collection on her honeymoon with Napoleon in Milan, with the captured Italian masterpieces as the nucleus. Patronizing the best artists of her day, she made a career of having her portrait painted—for her own and for Napoleon's walls, or as gifts for kings and kinfolk. Josephine's account books show forty portraits of herself purchased in the years 1812–14.

Malmaison's art treasures were open to guests, but very few were admitted to the sanctuary, Napoleon's old apartments, which were preserved exactly as they had been the day he left them: his guns, his swords, his maps, his desk with a history book left open at the page he had been reading. "One expected to see him enter at any moment into those rooms which he had abandoned forever," one guest noted. No one but Josephine could touch or dust what she called her "relics."

After the Emperor's remarriage, months at a time would go by without his paying a visit to the old Empress at Malmaison, for the new Empress was so jealous that he had to go secretly, without her knowledge.

Just when Josephine thought "The Emperor has forgotten me completely!" as she wrote in a letter to Eugene in the spring of 1812, just then Napoleon drove in to visit, to sit for "two whole hours with her," as one of her ladies in waiting described the scene, "on the circular bench under the tulip tree."

It is unlikely that Josephine would have understood—had Napoleon tried to explain at the time of his visit to her—his reasons for the campaign he was about to launch against Russia. It may have been his old dream of a United States of Europe that was driving him into the Russian steppes. It may have been because the Czar of Russia refused to stand with him any longer against England, or because he had discovered that Russia and Prussia had just signed a secret treaty. Or it may have been that he felt a showdown with Russia was inevitable, that "one more good battle" would change the face of the world and assure him mastery of it.

Whatever Napoleon's reasons, they were wrong. He was making a serious mistake; France would suffer her first reverses in nearly twenty years.

The Russians could not stand and fight Napoleon's superior forces; instead, they retreated, burning the fields and crops, the towns and cities and storehouses behind them as they went.

The golden cupolas of Moscow glittered in the September sun, but Napoleon's entry into the Kremlin was an empty vic-

140

tory, for the Russian army was still intact, somewhere to the north or east. The city was as empty as the victory, bare of supplies, desolate, silent, smoldering with the fires set by the inhabitants before they fled.

Napoleon waited anxiously for a month for peace proposals from the Czar, but no Russian emissaries arrived—only early frosts and swirling snows. It was not the Russian Commander-in-Chief, General Kutusov, who defeated the French, it was "General Famine and General Winter," as one of the French officers lamented.

Josephine was filled with dark forebodings before the dreadful news ever reached her, news of the French army's retreat from Moscow: only fifty thousand men marching out of Russia where five hundred thousand had marched in.

Josephine would not learn until months later that Napoleon's crack troops, his Old Guard, had slogged west with her name on their frost-bitten lips: Our Lady of Victory, or the name they called her by now, The Old Empress. Superstitious, as soldiers often are, these veterans of Italy and Egypt grumbled as they crossed the frozen wastes (with wolves and Cossacks at their heels) that their Emperor should never have changed wives! That his *first* wife had brought him and them luck, whereas as much could not be said for the *second* wife: this first campaign since Napoleon's marriage to the Austrian woman had resulted in his and their first real defeat.

Once across the Russian border, the Emperor rushed by sleigh to Paris, to prevent a panic in the capital in the wake of the Empire's shattering military defeat.

He arrived at the Tuileries on December eighteenth at midnight and, late as the hour was, it did not seem to him too late to send a special courier to Josephine at Malmaison, to reassure her about himself and her son, Eugene.

"Thank God, my son is still alive!" she could write gratefully to Hortense, although she would not see Eugene again for months. He stayed on in Germany in command, regrouping the pitiful remnants, the bits and pieces of France's once proud, once invincible Grand Army.

After their defeat, France stood at bay, hemmed in by enemies: the English had joined the Spanish to hammer at France's southern border. Russia, Prussia, and Sweden were massing for an attack on France's northeastern frontier. Even Napoleon's father-in-law, the Emperor of Austria, even Eugene's father-in-law, the King of Bavaria, would join the coalition, and France would find herself standing alone against all Europe.

Sometime in the late winter or early spring of 1813, before he went to join Eugene and the army across the Rhine, Napoleon went to Malmaison to see Josephine. If she wept that day, after he had driven off, as she customarily did, she had cause for weeping. It would prove to be their final parting. He and she would never meet again.

142

Part V

Events went rushing toward disaster.

Just as suddenly as Napoleon's star had risen, it declined. If it was destiny which had raised him to the heights, it now dashed him down to the depths. The luck which had seemed to distinguish him for twenty years, now deserted him, overnight, as he and his men fought against odds of two to one, across Germany.

By the fall of the year 1813, the French army reeled in defeat, retreated west behind the Rhine. By December, France's enemies pursued the retreating French legions across that river, into France itself.

"Never before had such a panic seized the capital!" cried Hortense. "All the people of the north in league against us, finally set foot on sacred French soil . . . a shock to France, so long victorious, her borders so long inviolate."

Hortense went to Malmaison on the night of January 23, 1814, to describe the scene she had witnessed that morning in the Tuileries: Napoleon with the King of Rome in his arms, announcing his departure for headquarters, entrusting the regency of France to the Empress, and the defense of Paris to the National Guard.

The "sacred soil" of France which he had gone to defend inspired Napoleon to wage the most brilliant campaign of his entire career—and his men the most valiant of theirs. At the same time, however, it was the most hopeless and the most desperate of all the campaigns in which they had been engaged: three months of relentless warfare against overwhelming odds.

By March, calamity was upon them. Napoleon led his heroic French troops to incredible victories; then, hopelessly outnumbered, encircled, and outflanked, they retreated toward the besieged capital.

Lookouts on the towers of Notre Dame Cathedral were reporting that enemy columns could be seen marching on Paris. Yet, unbelieving, Josephine was writing to Hortense: "This must be one of the Emperor's maneuvers which we cannot understand. He is not the man to allow himself to be taken by surprise. He will come at the moment when he is least expected and save the capital."

Not this time. Napoleon could produce no miracle from under his cocked hat, such as everyone expected.

No one, least of all, Josephine, could believe that the Emperor could be defeated, that Paris could fall.

Hortense was shocked at the roar of the cannon as the Russians and Prussians advanced on the city. "Until then, I had heard cannon fired only at victory celebrations," she wrote sadly. And she was stunned when Marie Louise, the Regent, and Prince Joseph, head of the Council, decided to abandon the capital, to withdraw to the south to the safety of the Loire River valley—with the King of Rome and all the imperial family.

144

Part V

As the forces of the allied invaders converged on Paris, and the French imperial family packed its treasures and made ready to evacuate the Tuileries Palace, Josephine found herself isolated at Malmaison. As she wrote her daughter, she was alone there with with her staff and "with a guard of only sixteen men—and these, disabled war veterans." The Empress-Regent, Marie Louise, never gave a thought to her predecessor, the ex-Empress Josephine; it was Hortense who, on March twenty-eighth, finally sent a message to her mother to set out instantly for her château in Normandy.

Josephine readied herself quickly, her maid helping her to sew her diamonds and pearls into the lining of the quilted skirt she would wear on the journey.

At her château of Navarre, Josephine waited in an agony of suspense for some word from her children, from the Emperor. "Only news from you can console me," she wrote to Hortense on March thirty-first, "I have never lacked courage to meet the many perilous situations in which I have found myself during my life, and I should always be able to meet reverses of fortune with equanimity, but what I cannot endure is this separation from my children, this uncertainty as to their fate."

What a relief to Josephine to see her daughter and two little grandsons drive up to her door on April first!

Although Hortense and Josephine had not yet heard the news, the Coalition troops, led by the Czar Alexander, had marched into Paris the day before, March thirty-first. Napoleon had been repudiated, deposed by the French Senate; with most of his army gone and his generals deserting, he had had no choice but to abdicate, to give up all claim to his crown and his empire, proposing that they be transferred to his son, the King of Rome. But the Russians, the Prussians, and the English turned down that proposal; they preferred a Bourbon to a Bonaparte, and restored that ancient line of kings to the French throne in the person of Louis XVIII, a brother of Louis XVI who had died on the guillotine. Louis XVI's only son, who would have been Louis XVII, had died or disappeared in prison during the Revolution—no one ever really knew what had happened to the little boy.

Napoleon's son would have been Napoleon II, had he succeeded his father. Instead, the child was to go with his mother to Austria, where he would be known as the Duke of Reichstadt . . . not much of a title for a boy, who at his birth, had been proclaimed King of Rome, and who would die in Vienna, in 1832, at age twenty-one, in the palace of his grandfather, the Austrian Emperor. (When a Bonaparte finally recovered the throne of France, in 1851, it was Napoleon III, the great Napoleon's nephew, youngest son of Hortense and Louis, grandson of Josephine.)

The great Napoleon himself, however, was sent into exile by his conquerors, to the island of Elba, a tiny dot six miles off the coast of Italy—a kingdom of eighty-six square miles for the former Emperor of France, dictator of Europe.

When the news reached Josephine she threw herself into Hortense's arms, crying: "Oh, that poor Napoleon! How dreadful for him! Were it not for his wife, I would go join him in exile!"

"It was then I saw how much she still loved him," Hortense wrote. "As we learned the details of the national catastrophe, it was above all the fate of the Emperor which grieved my Mother."

"I am heartbroken at the way they have treated the Emperor," Josephine wrote to her son. She was proud that Eugene had stood by his stepfather, loyal to the end.

Napoleon wrote to Josephine before his departure into exile:

My fall is great, but it will serve a useful purpose. . . . In the retreat into which I am going, I shall substitute the pen for the sword. The history of my reign will make a curious one. . . . Adieu, my dear Josephine. Resign yourself to fate, as I have done, and never forget him who has never forgotten you . . . and never will.

The Czar of Russia sent a message to Josephine to assure her that she and her children would be shown every courtesy and honor by him and by the other European monarchs occupying Paris.

She returned from Normandy in mid-April, at tulip time, when Malmaison was at its loveliest. The famous rose gardens were in bud, but she was not to live to see them bloom, that spring of 1814.

She was very melancholy. Napoleon's fate distressed her, and she worried about her children's future which, until so recently, had seemed so bright. They would not, she knew, be welcome at a Bourbon court, in a Bourbon France. What land could they call home? Were they doomed to be hapless wanderers, asking refuge here and there?

Then Josephine was suddenly stricken with what seemed to be a chill, a sore throat. Her voice was husky, her chest congested, but she would not give in to illness. The Czar and the Grand Dukes of Russia were expected at Malmaison, the King and Crown Prince of Prussia were on their way to call on the former Empress of France who must be on hand, splendorously gowned and bejewelled—her famous charming self—to receive them.

But the symptoms worsened; the doctors diagnosed "a putrid fever"—it was probably diphtheria—and she took to her

148

bed, her beautiful golden bed shaped like a swan, the swan which had been her emblem.

The artist Redouté, known as the rose painter, left his brushes and easel in the rose garden to go to Josephine's door to inquire about her, but she waved him away—as she had even her grandchildren—for fear her fever might be contagious.

Claire de Rémusat found Josephine elegant even in her illness, "dressed in rose-colored satin, all lacy and beribboned."

Within days, her condition grew critical.

Her son and daughter stood close by. Hortense thought she heard her mother speak the words: "Bonaparte . . . Elba . . . King of Rome . . ." If so, they were spoken with her last breath.

Her son wrote to his wife that his mother had gone "as sweetly and gently to meet death as she had met life."

The former Empress's body lay in state for three days, on a raised platform in the Malmaison entrance hall, marble-floored, black on white, with tall alabaster columns marking its graceful oval outline. Twenty thousand people filed past.

Josephine had, years earlier, converted this hall in to an aviary, filling it with bright-hued tropical birds—cockateels and cockatoos, macaws and parakeets—a gay and lively place with its flutter and flurry and whirr of wings, its flashes of brilliant plumage, its shrill bird cries. Now the birds had been banished from their perches, the bird song stilled and, instead, there came the toll of bells, all the church bells of the parish tolling day and night in a dirge for the onetime Empress. Now, all was gloom and shadow: the walls, from floor to ceiling, were draped in black, lit only by the eery flicker of a thousand candles burning around the bier—the aviary turned into a funeral chapel for Josephine-Rose-Yeyette, Bird of the Islands.

Frances Mossiker researched the life of Josephine Bonaparte in France for many months, reading original documents and visiting historical sites, such as the lovely Malmaison where the ex-Empress spent her last years.

A graduate of Barnard and Smith, Mrs. Mossiker lives in Dallas, Texas. As an author of adult books, she has written *The Queen's Necklace, The Affair of the Poisons,* and *Napoleon and Josephine—The Biography of a Marriage.*

Text set in Granjon
Composed by H. Wolff Book Mfg. Co., New York, N.Y.
Printed by Halliday Lithograph Corp., Hanover, Massachusetts
Bound by Montauk Book Manufacturing Co., Inc.,
Harrison, New Jersey
Typography by Thomas Morley